CHAPPALS TO HEELS

BHAVANA SINGH

Published By

Invincible Publication Pvt. Ltd.

Published by

Invincible Publication Pvt. Ltd.
201A, SAS Tower, Sector 38, Gurugram – 122003
Phone: +91-124-4034247, +91 9599066061
www.invinciblepublishers.com

Sales: Office No. 4760-61/23 Basement, Pratap Street,
Ansari Road, Daryaganj, Near ICICI Bank - 110002
Phone: +91-11-40198405
Email: invinciblepublishers@gmail.com

First edition – 2024

ISBN: 978-93-58861-76-1

CONTENTS

CHAPTER 1

Stitching the story of Bhavana Singh

When I first ran away from my home at the age of 16, I was a poor small town girl, who got off the bus wearing "purane kapde"(old clothes) and some worn out pair of chappals. I had nothing with me but just the eyes full of dreams and the courage of a warrior. I call this my sassy chappal phase, because at that time even though I didn't come from money, I was all alone in a big city, no support, no guidance, nothing; but these chappals, they helped me walk towards the life of my dreams. The journey from here to my beloved heels was a long and a tiring one. There were many stops, many stumbles, many challenges that pushed me to the ground so many times but ultimately I did manage to walk the city with the most powerful sound in my world, the tick-tock of my high fashion heels.

Clothes, fashion, fabric, designs, was my share of magic. The art of fashion, it gave me the purpose to live, to face each adversity and overcome it. It was the dream you know, a boss lady walking tall in her heels carrying a luxury tote bag with the confidence that has been crafted with the trials of her life, with her hard work, all paving way for her never ending courage.

At the age of 16, I had also opened my first clothing store. It was the beginning of a young girl's journey, born into poverty, but who wanted to make it big in the fashion world. At that time, I was working as a waitress in one of the famous restaurant chains, where I would wait tables, clean dishes and work day and night to survive for my life. Even while I was washing those dishes, listening to people complain about their food, my mind was always thinking about the dream. It didn't let me sleep, I would always be restless but you know I was "good restless". It was like a fire that burnt inside, a fire that was meant to take me ahead in life, that was meant to show me light someday. After a few months of working here, I took out some loan on my salary and invested it in my clothing store. That day I was the happiest I had been in the 15 years of my life.

In one of his interviews, Mr. Shah Rukh Khan said, "in the times when you are the loneliest, it's your art that gives you the purpose to live." I was a mere 16 year old girl, I had no one to support me but I had my art, a dream related to that art and courage of a warrior. I am not boasting about myself, or writing this book to eulogize my life's journey. Rather I want to tell you that dreams empower you to overcome any problem, they empower you to become the best version of yourself and create your reality on your own terms. I want my life to be an example for people who are on their journeys, waiting for their tables to turn and especially to those who love fashion as much as me.

I'll tell you something, fashion is actually considered to be a very shallow profession, something that is all about the external; beauty, makeup, style, materialism and it's not considered as a profession that adds real value to the society. But fashion for me has been the sole purpose of my life, I breathed it, I lived it and I am alive because of it. In times where I had no one, no friend, no partner, it was my art that would feel like a hug on a bad day, that felt like a companion on a lonely night and as light in the worst of the dark phases. Looking back, I know that this was what I was meant to do, meant to be and this path has guided me throughout. When there is no light outside, you have to search for it within you. You have to become the lamp for yourself. And this was where it all started. I struggled, and I struggled a lot, things never came easy for me. Time always tested my patience, my dreams tested my determination, my relationships tested my love, and my art tested my courage. But to be honest, if none of the trials had been there, I wouldn't have even been half of what I am today. And not just career wise but as a person, my journey has made me appreciate the value of everything I receive, it has made me understand that the biggest gift is the breath we hold, it has given me the depth to understand the world, to be grateful and most importantly to be happy in my life.

Growing up my family didn't have a lot of money; to be honest, we didn't have any money. There was no emotional support, no sweet memories, each of us was fighting the brutal battle of survival. As a child, I saw the worst of adversities, we lived in a hand-to-mouth situation, there was no scope of becoming something better than what we were. I would be asked to leave the classroom and stand outside as a form of punishment because my parents had defaulted to pay my fee. Then being asked "my rates" as a mere teenager, a vulnerable girl who didn't even know what those words meant. Then working as a maid at my teacher's place so that I could somehow just pay for my basic schooling. It was hard, I still get goosebumps thinking about the contrast that I have lived through in my past. While my life was in the shadows of the shadows, while I was being made fun of at school for my entire essence, for where I came from, the kind of clothes I wore; my pretty little head never stopped dreaming. There was a loud strong voice that always told me, "Bhavana you are meant to do big things, don't give up, don't you ever give up." And then I dusted off each remark, each attack on my identity, each brutality and I would get up again, ready to fight another day.

"Thump thump thump" the sound of a moving sewing machine, the snip of a pair of scissors cutting at the fresh fabric, all working out to execute a design, everything hyping up to build a beautiful item of cloth. This was all I ever wanted. Since I was a child, my dreamland was where my tools were. I think I was born a stylist, a designer. Back then even though we didn't have money, but whatever little we had, some scattered, leftover pieces of clothes, I would patch them up and try to create something out of it. Or try to style whatever worn out clothes I had because that's all my mind knew. It only knew art, it only knew fashion, it only knew clothes. My mind was working through the messes of life but my heart was always there around clothes, it was always conspiring to make me an artist. As soon as I hit teenage, things at my home started getting even more difficult so I ran away from my place. When I came to Delhi I hopped off the bus with no backup, no resources, my feet were restlessly walking on a pair of worn out 'chappals', and this is where my 'chappals to heels' journey started. And then as I said I started working as a waitress. It was here that I gathered the resources and little loaned capital to open a small shop. I can't even tell you the pride I felt when my small business, this small shop established by a young girl, started actually doing good. I ran the shop for a few years and fast forward to a few years ahead; my life's plans changed and I got married. When a girl moves to her in-laws house after marriage, she packs her life into suitcases, and takes it along with her to the husband's house. Her life packs into small little compartments and her entire stronghold changes. I too had packed my life, through this transition and it all fitted into just two bags. After I arrived at my in-laws place, there were a few relatives who sat around that evening, wanting to see the riches I had brought from my 'maika'. And then one of them asked me to show what I had brought with me. My father-in-law saw me hesitating and immediately he put down this request, saying "whatever is in these bags is hers, no one has the right to see or ask to see the content of it". And now I think, somehow my in-laws already had an idea that whatever I had packed in those bags was 'nothing', it was my empty life. And they chose to protect me. For the first time in a very long time, the little girl inside me, had felt free, safe and happy. So, now that I had a place to call home, I redirected the focus on my career. Back at my place, I had handed over my shop to my brother so that even though I would be gone, this beautiful thing that I built with my own hands would be safe with my family. But to establish business elsewhere was hard and doing it alone without capital, without resources would have been like going back to square one. So, I decided to ask my husband for help and offered him an idea to open the same store at his place. After a lot of pondering, calculating, and analyzing he finally agreed to give my idea a chance and luckily the plan worked out, a few months in and the business started doing really well. My husband and I were very happy but you know this was not it. It was a few months into the workings of this store that the same inner voice whispered again. "We can't stop here, life is waiting for the next challenge." I decided to work towards building something of my own, my husband gradually fell in love with the store we had built together, so we decided that he would handle this business and I would continue to chase my dreams.

Throughout my journey, I have fallen a lot many times but I want to tell you something, I have always considered myself as God's favorite child. I know that adversities have been like shadows in my life. I have cried with wrenching howls over the mishappenings, felt like giving up so many times even to a point where I fell deep into the pit of depression but God was always there. He was there in one form or another. And I know that we are busy planning the next step, God would be up there making the bigger, the better master plan for us. God gave me trials and tribulations, so that I could become this version of myself today. He gave me tests but he also gave me strength, he gave me darkness but also faith, and it is always in the worst of your phases that you find the most of your strength.

I was listening to a podcast recently, and I heard one of the guests say that the right amount of trauma in your early part of life sets the stage for success in the latter. Given the right mix of it, your success becomes proportional to the hardships that you have faced early on. God gave me opportunities and setbacks as he gave me courage and passion to follow through. I fell down but I always felt God's protection was over me because of which I gathered the courage to stand up each time. And this is why each failure awakened a force, a determination inside me. I was always trying to think of ways with which I could finance my business, "what's gonna be the next step Bhavana", "think think, where are you going to get money from?", "it's not over until you call it off", "our dream is not dead yet". I wanted to start with the next phase of my business plan but there was no money and I didn't know where I would get it from. My husband had already invested in the shop and i was too embarrassed to ask anyone else for money. Besides I didn't have anyone else to ask for money. So, I was just sitting there, surrounded by my own set of tribulations, and I caught sight of this shining piece of jewelry that hung down my neck. I saw my Mangalsutra. The business woman inside me saw it as a capital that I could stake to build my dream and the wife inside me would not let me do anything to this endearing piece of her jewelry. I fought with myself inside for the remaining time, only to get up the next day, go straight to the jewelry shop and then stake whatever I had, for whatever I wanted in the future.

Nobody knew about this but it was a chance I was ready to take. I thought to myself it's mine, it's my property and I need it now so I shall use it. I don't know what to make of this even today, sometimes I laugh as to how crazy I was, and sometimes I just feel amazed as to what drove this passion inside, only god shall know.

Luckily, the money I got from this emotional treadmill, laid the foundation of whatever I have today. My growth started with it and I built my path to reach the next ladders in my career. Moving ahead, climbing each hill one by one, I started to build my life around my passion.

I'll tell you one thing, your art, your passion, is not an isolated event that happens in absence of everything. It's not like your life and your passion are two different things. You work and then you follow your passion, you go about your life and then you work on your art. This segregation doesn't work when you want your dreams, your art to manifest in your life. You have to become one with it. It leaves you restless everyday, it leaves you sleepless every night, you think it while eating, while sleeping, it's like love. You have to embody the spirit of it and immerse yourself in its realization. And this happened to me. I would try to dress in style always, it was in my nature to put effort into my dressing, into my clothes. I embodied the spirit of a stylist (not literally though, I was not possessed). And everything about me was correlated to fashion, to style.

And people would notice it, they asked me where I had bought those clothes, where I learnt to dress like that or how I designed what I wore. One day a woman messaged me saying, "I love the way you style your clothes, how much would you charge to style me as well?" I went blank for a moment because I had never thought that this skill, this hobby of mine could turn into money. "My knack for styling could be monetized?"I asked myself this.

Even though it took quite a few hours to wrap my head around what this woman was asking of me, I went ahead and told her that I would charge her some 5,000 rupees per month for the same. To my surprise this woman agreed to pay me. It's been some ten years and she is still one of my clients. Even today, I style her and given that she was where it all started, our arrangement still stands at the same terms till today. She calls herself my lucky charm. And if you are reading this, I would never deny the fact that your initiation actually laid the foundation to my future and you in fact have been my lucky charm.

Few more clients, and being a stylist became my thing. I actually became a stylist. I started walking into the path of my childhood dream. When I was reaching there, I could see the silver lining. The wait, the hardwork and the patience was finally paying off. What I had endured for my life was finally coming to show results. And to my surprise it was happening in the form that I didn't even know off. I didn't know you could make money by styling people. I didn't know that what I thought was a mere hobby was actually employable. People needed someone who could understand fashion and style.

And I think it all happened because I became one with my art. It became an intrinsic part of my life and me that everyone around can see that I am in my real sense what I work for. Through my journey, I have learnt that when you don't understand fashion, you try to fit every body into the narrow definition of beauty, of what looks good. Besides there being varying shapes, sizes and colors of bodies and our faces, we only appreciate one kind of beauty. But a person who understands fashion, they see beyond the usual, their sense of fashion and style gives them the creativity to see beauty for what it is, it's unique and diverse at the same time. Fashion is freedom. Without this sense, the world only knows a crammed up definition of beauty. For real intelligence to kick in you need creativity, you need fashion you need freedom. It's not just about clothes, about makeup, it's an expression of you as a person. What colors you like, what clothes you like, what designs you like, they are not superficial sets of data, they are entry points into the real you.

What my life taught me, gave me an unique edge in this industry. I can create a balance between the macroscopic and microscopic because I have lived fashion. And this skill I embodied was spotted by the head at Promenade in one of my guest lectures at their facility and he being the great man he is, offered me to work there as the Style Director at DLF promenade. I have learnt a lot during those five years that I worked there, gathered a lot of professional insights into the cut and stitch world, into the beauty world and this, along with my life's learnings, is what I am passing on through this book. As Bhavana Singh, a crazy passionate fashion enthusiast, whatever I have learnt through my journey about fashion and styling fundamentals, I think it's time to share it with the young people who are aspiring to be the future of this industry.

CHAPTER 2

Understanding features, personality and flaws

Indian make-up is mostly inspired by Bollywood. Most women follow their favorite actors/ actresses and try to replicate their hairstyle, dresses and make-up.

When I start working with a client, I always ask them who is their role model in fashion, or who is it that they look up to for fashion inspiration. Their answer says a lot about the kind of person they are and the style makeover that I need to follow through. For example if a girl tells me that her fashion icon is Deepika padukone, I would decipher that she would be more inclined towards sophisticated, powerful looks for herself. If she says Alia Bhatt, I would understand her nature to be bubbly and more on the cute, pretty styles. Besides the obvious, each person has a unique blend of facial features, personality, body language and their life's story. You cannot see them in segregation or else you might fail to develop a style which in the most original sense suits the individual. Fashion as I said is beyond the superficial. It is a depth of an artist's vision that should be utilized to bring the best in a person. Before you even begin to choose the right clothing and fashion style for yourself, you should first understand what is your personality, and if you are styling someone else, start with first observing them as a whole being. I'll expand more on my mantra of styling in the next chapter but for this one let's develop on the fundamentals first.

The fundamentals lie in the structure of the body, the color of the skin, the attributes and largely in the body language. Your first focus should be in understanding how thc features of the face work together to build or break style. You shall never try to fit your clients, or yourself into narrow definitions of body types. Each body is different and it should be styled keeping the uniqueness in mind. I acknowledge that there are certain traits that are similar in body types but nobody would even want to listen to you telling them, "you are a pear shaped body and should choose these and avoid these." Don't constrict them in rules but help them to play around those rules so that they can learn to wear their preferences in the best taste.

Getting back, the first attribute I always pick while styling someone is the hair color. And let me start with it first.

1. Hair color

The choice of hair color is determined by the skin tone of a person. If you have a warmer skin tone, you always go with warmer hair colors. If you have a cool skin tone, you go with cool color tones. Hair color can be chosen to complement the color of the eyes. For example, certain hair colors can make eye color pop or create a harmonious balance. Consideration of both warm and cool tones in hair color can enhance the eyes. Styles that brighten and lift the eyes can contribute to a more youthful and radiant appearance. Techniques such as highlights or updos can create a lifting effect, drawing attention to the eyes and creating a refreshed look. Stylists can use their expertise to recommend hairstyles that address specific eye-related concerns, such as minimizing the appearance of under-eye bags or dark circles, or working with particular eye shapes.

But what are skin tones and how to determine it?

As a stylist, understanding your client's skin tone is crucial for recommending the most flattering hair color. Skin tone refers to the natural color of a person's skin, and it is categorized into various undertones, warm, cool, or neutral.

Undertones:

- **Cool Undertones:** People with cool undertones have hints of blue, pink, or purple in their skin.
- **Warm Undertones:** Warm undertones have hints of yellow, peach, or gold in the skin.
- **Neutral Undertones:** Individuals with neutral undertones have a balanced mix of warm and cool tones in their skin.

Look at the veins on the inside of your wrist under natural light. If they appear more blue, you likely have cool undertones. If they appear more green, you likely have warm undertones. If you have difficulty determining the dominant color, you may have neutral undertones. Hold a piece of white fabric and then a beige fabric near your face. If the white fabric complements your skin more, you likely have cool undertones. If the beige fabric looks better, you likely have warm undertones. Your client's natural hair and eye color can also provide clues. Cool undertones often accompany blue or gray eyes and blonde, brown, or black hair with ash tones. Warm undertones are commonly associated with brown or hazel eyes and hair in shades of red, auburn, or warm brown. Consider how your client's skin reacts to sunlight. If they tend to burn easily and have difficulty tanning, they may have cool undertones. If they tan easily and rarely burn, they likely have warm undertones.

How to decide hair color based on your skin tone?

Choosing the right hair color based on your skin tone can significantly enhance your overall appearance. Here's a guide to help you decide on the most flattering hair color for your skin tone:

Determine Your Skin Tone:

☆ **Cool Undertones:**

- **Indicators:** Veins on your wrist appear blue. You look better in silver jewelry.
- **Colors that Suit You:** Cool shades like ash brown, platinum blonde, cool black, and icy tones.

☆ **Warm Undertones:**

- **Indicators:** Veins on your wrist appear green. Gold jewelry complements your skin.

- **Colors that Suit You:** Warm tones such as golden blonde, caramel brown, copper, and warm reds.

☆ **Neutral Undertones:**

- **Indicators:** You can wear both silver and gold jewelry. Your veins appear blue-green.
- **Colors that Suit You:** You have the flexibility to experiment with both cool and warm tones.

Matching Hair Color to Skin Tone:

☆ **For Cool Undertones:**

- **Hair Colors:** Cool shades like platinum, ash blonde, ash brown, cool black, and silver. Avoid overly warm tones that may clash with your cool undertones.

☆ **For Warm Undertones:**

- **Hair Colors:** Warm tones such as golden blonde, honey brown, auburn, and copper. Steer clear of overly cool tones that may make you look washed out.

☆ **For Neutral Undertones:**

- **Hair Colors:** You have the versatility to

choose from both warm and cool tones. Experiment with colors like chestnut brown, neutral blonde, or a mix of warm and cool highlights.

Consider Your Natural Color:

☆ **Going Darker:**

- If you have a fair complexion, going too dark might create too much contrast. Consider rich browns and medium tones.
- If you have a darker complexion, you can pull off deeper, darker shades.

☆ **Going Lighter:**

- Lighter shades can complement fair skin tones, but be cautious not to go too light, as it might wash you out.
- Medium to light shades often work well for medium and olive skin tones.
- Darker skin tones can explore a wide range of light to medium shades without looking overly stark.

Test with Temporary Colors:

☆ Wig or Clip-In Extensions:

- Try on wigs or clip-in extensions in different shades to get a visual of how the color interacts with your skin tone before committing.

☆ Temporary Hair Dyes:

- Experiment with temporary or semi-permanent hair dyes to test how the color looks and feels on you. This allows you to make adjustments without a long-term commitment.

Seek Professional Advice:

☆ Consult a Stylist:

- A professional stylist can analyze your skin tone, consider your personal style, and recommend the most suitable hair color.

☆ Consider Maintenance:

- Discuss maintenance levels with your stylist. Some colors require more upkeep than others, so choose a shade that aligns with your willingness to maintain the color.

2. Facial features

2.1 Eyes

As a stylist, the eyes are a crucial feature to consider when working with clients. They play an important role in expressing emotion, and the depth of one's life. I always see that if a client doesn't look directly into my eyes while talking, it shows the lack of confidence and some form of hesitation in connection. This is why fashion cannot be just about connecting on the outside with the client, cannot be just about recommending only the clothes or makeup but about finding the base with which you can connect with them from within. It is about knowing them as a person and eyes are a door to it.

If we go on the technical side, eyes are the focal point of the face. When you have worked on styling the hair, with the right hairstyle and hair color it will draw attention towards eyes. The eyes play a key role in balancing facial features. Stylists often work with clients to shape and define eyebrows, which can have a significant impact on the overall appearance of the eyes. Well-groomed eyebrows compliment the eyes and contribute to a polished look. Stylists can recommend styles that align with the client's personality and desired level of expression through their eyes. The eyes provide a versatile canvas for styling. Different makeup techniques, eyewear, and hairstyles can be used to create diverse looks that highlight the eyes for various occasions. Recognizing the uniqueness of each client's eyes allows for personalized styling recommendations. Tailoring hairstyles to accentuate their eye shape and color contributes to an individualized and stylish appearance. When clients feel that their eyes are beautifully highlighted, it can boost their confidence and contribute to a positive self-image. Stylists have the opportunity to empower clients by enhancing features that are central to their identity.

Starting with the features first let me explain styling to you

☆ **Face Shape:**

- **Features:** Forehead, cheekbones, jawline, and chin.
- **Styling Impact:** Different face shapes suit different hairstyles and accessories.

For example, round faces may benefit from angular hairstyles, while oval faces are versatile and can carry various styles effectively. Accessories like earrings and glasses can be chosen to complement or balance the face shape.

☆ **Identifying Face Shapes:**

- Common face shapes include oval, round, square, heart, diamond, and long. Determine the client's face shape by examining the width and length of their face, as well as the prominence of certain features.

☆ **Oval Face Shape:**

- An oval face is with balanced proportions. Most styles complement an oval face. However, it's essential to maintain balance and avoid overwhelming the face with excessive volume.

☆ **Round Face Shape:**

- Round faces benefit from styles that add angles and definition. Long, layered hairstyles and clothing with vertical lines can elongate the appearance of the face. Avoid overly round hairstyles and opt for those that add height and length.

☆ **Square Face Shape:**

- Square faces often have a strong jawline. Softening the angles with layered hairstyles, soft waves, and rounded necklines in clothing can help balance the features. Avoid overly geometric or boxy shapes.

☆ **Heart Face Shape:**

- Heart-shaped faces have a broader forehead and a narrower jawline. Styles that balance the width of the forehead with the jaw, such as shoulder-length hair or A-line dresses, work well. Soft, flowing fabrics can complement this face shape.

☆ **Diamond Face Shape:**

- Diamond faces have a narrow forehead and jawline with wider cheekbones. Styles that soften the angles, such as layered haircuts and open-neckline clothing, can enhance this face shape. Avoid overly wide or pointy designs.

☆ **Body Shape:**

- You must have heard of the very commonly used terms like hourglass, peach body, rectangle shape, inverted triangle and stylists often bring down their client's to fit into these narrow categorizations of shapes. understanding one's body shape guides the selection of clothing styles. Hourglass figures can emphasize their curves with fitted dresses, while pear shapes might opt for A-line skirts to balance proportions. Tailored clothing enhances the silhouette, and strategic choices create a visually appealing look. I have never ever gone into describing my clients as body types, because I myself don't like the confines of body type segregations rather I go by my own theory. what are your best features, what accentuates your color tone and what compliments your body's figure? And when someone comes up to me mentioning and describing their flaws, I take note to show to them that these are not flaws rather certain hints that a stylist must develop onto. It is my job to use your features to bring out the best in you. It's not my job to highlight your flaws and then beat you down with it. For me flaws do not exist, it's just that each body is different and it needs to be styled in its own unique way. This is what I look into. I have seen people of all ages picking and choosing just out of the shelf, thinking what looks good on others might also compliment their body. Some choose style to cover what hides inside; shame and humiliation from being called out for the way their bodies are, to these people a stylist's job is to use their uniqueness to create art, to develop fashion that fits their bodies not to trigger those traumas again and make them conscious about their looks. Your each part of the body is an asset that can be used to build a fashionable look for you. Starting from your eyes, to something that is considered vestigial as nails, can be used as a canvas to create a work of art through you. A stylists canvas is the body itself, our art is YOU.

☆ **Posture and Body Language:**

- Body posture is a fundamental aspect that significantly influences personal style. Beyond its impact on physical structure, how one carries themselves can make or break the overall impression of their chosen fashion.

- Let's say if you are wearing clothes that are meant to portray you in power, a bad posture can bring the overall appearance to a mere facade, signifying that you might be pretending to look a certain way. Maintaining good posture exudes confidence and presence, which actually are the key elements that enhance the effectiveness of any style. Clothes fit better when draped on a body with proper posture, avoiding awkward bunching or pulling. Posture also affects the perception of body proportions, with an upright stance often creating a more balanced and visually appealing silhouette. Comfort and wearability also hinge on posture; feeling at ease in one's clothing is essential for genuine confidence. In professional settings, good posture is associated with professionalism and contributes to a polished image. Also, body language, conveyed through posture, can give hints about mood, attitude, and approachability. Body posture is a subtle tool but no doubt a powerful one in the art of personal styling, influencing not only the physical presentation of clothing but also the overall impact and perception of an individual.

- **Features:** Body alignment and gestures.
- **Styling Impact:** Confidence and posture contribute significantly to personal style. Standing tall and carrying oneself with confidence can enhance the overall impression. Additionally, the way clothing fits and drapes on the body can be influenced by posture.

☆ **Personal Style Preferences:**

- As stylists we ought to balance the aspects of what we think is right for the client and what they want. Personal style preferences are all about that. As I mentioned earlier also, I first ask my client, which celebrity's style do they gravitate towards the most. And their choices hold a lot of information as to who it is that they would like to look like. It's their vision too that we need to be considerate about. Once you learn the subtleties of a client's preference you can either match them with these styles, or use your own creativity to build a wardrobe that is inspired by a combination of your expertise and their personal preferences.

- Some people like Timeless and elegant, classic style. It involves neutral colors, well-tailored pieces, and simple lines. Some like to go with the free-spirited and eclectic vibe of bohemian style which embraces flowy fabrics, bold patterns, and a mix of accessories for a relaxed, artistic look. Some are Inspired street style which adorns casual and comfortable clothing with elements that have relation to sports and hip-hop fashion. Some are minimalists, clean lines, simple silhouettes, and a limited color palette define their style preference. You can mix and match or stick to what you and client think is best for them.

- **Features:** Individual preferences in colors, patterns, and styles.

- **Styling Impact:** Personal style is a culmination of preferences. Whether one gravitates towards minimalist or eclectic styles, or warm or cool tones, understanding personal preferences helps in curating a wardrobe that resonates with individual tastes and values.

CHAPTER 3

My style mantra

G Given that you build an understanding and then work on the basics of styling, eventually based on your life experiences, work exposures and your own personal dispositions, you'll develop a particular way of doing things. I too have a process and a way with which I work in my creative zone, this is what I call my style mantra.

Broadly, there are two types of projects that a stylist majorly works upon in their career. One is the reel world, where models, actors, actresses are required to be styled for particular roles or shoots. Here a stylist presents a certain look for commercial or artistic reasons. However, the other side of the story is with people from real walks of life. My work mostly revolves around this sphere. See, I am a firm believer in the fact that clothes or any style for that matter cannot hide what is inside. If you try to hide what is inside of you with style and clothes that do not align with your personality, you are just putting a facade on the world. It simply shows how underconfident a person is about themselves. Each personality can be enhanced and brought to its true aspects with fashion. I am again saying, fashion is not just about what looks good on the outside, it is about how the inner self of a person is expressed using the art and definition of clothing. Each aspect of an individual's personality needs to be accommodated to create a style that suits the person you are working with.

I'll give you an example. Imagine you're working with a client who is naturally introverted, they express themselves through simple creativity rather than bold statements. They will feel comfortable in clothes that match their personality and prefer a more minimalist style. On the other hand, in the "reel world", a stylist might even succeed in pulling off a more extroverted or glamorous look on the same person.

So, in your approach, which focuses on the real world and aligning style with the individual's personality, you would consider the introverted nature of your client. Instead of pushing them into outfits that may seem glamorous and don't resonate with their inner self, you might opt for more subdued and artistic clothing. Perhaps, you choose pieces that allow them to express their creativity subtly, like well-crafted accessories, unique textures, or colors that resonate with their artistic side.

By doing so, you not only enhance their appearance but also ensure that their style aligns with their personality, fostering a sense of authenticity. This approach goes beyond just the outer appearance and aims to bring out the true essence of the individual through their clothing choices.

My style mantra is based on the inward-outward approach. I largely work with people that are working men and women. And for them, styling is not just about clothes, most often than not, their need for a makeover stems from a story that is either related to a past trauma or a realization that they have let too much time go because they didn't choose themselves first. To these people, the answer is never outward, it is not in the material or the color palette of their wardrobe. It lies deep within themselves and when they turn to me for help, I know my duty goes way beyond giving them a choice of clothing. Always know this, in life the "why" of doing something is the most important question. When your reason is strong enough your result will surely manifest. This is why my process is to always and always start with the "why". I first spend my time observing what is the reason why my client has turned towards a makeover. Their goals, their vision and their likes and dislikes, can be pretty much understood with this first layer of bonding.

The moment you understand the "why", the moment you delve into the story and you become a companion for your client to take on the forthcoming journey, you open them to experimentation and change. Once I understand this point of view and the place that the person is coming from, I can now build on the next layer, which is, understanding their schedules and routines. The distribution of their time and their routines, the kind of work the person does, is key to building their style. And this is where my **time capsule wardrobe** comes in.

What is a time capsule wardrobe?

A time capsule wardrobe refers to a collection of essential, timeless, and versatile pieces of clothing that can be mixed and matched to create a variety of outfits. The concept is to have a curated selection of high-quality, classic items that withstand changing fashion trends and can be worn over an extended period.

The goal of a time capsule wardrobe is to simplify one's closet, making it more efficient and reducing the need for frequent shopping. By investing in key pieces that are both durable and stylish, individuals can create a wardrobe that stands the test of time, transitioning seamlessly between seasons and occasions.

☆ **Typically, a time capsule wardrobe includes items like:**

- **Classic White Shirt:** Versatile and can be dressed up or down.
- **Well-fitted Jeans:** A timeless and comfortable staple.
- **Tailored Blazer:** Adds a touch of sophistication to various outfits.
- **Little Black Dress (LBD):** Suitable for a range of formal or semi-formal occasions.

- **Neutral-Colored Trench Coat:** Timeless outerwear that works in different seasons.
- **Quality Leather Shoes:** Classic footwear that complements various outfits.
- **White Sneakers:** Casual, comfortable, and versatile.
- **Neutral-Colored Sweater:** Provides warmth and pairs well with different bottoms.
- **A-Line Skirt or Chinos:** Versatile bottoms that can be dressed up or down.
- **Classic Accessories:** Timeless pieces like a quality watch or a versatile handbag.

The idea is to have a wardrobe that is cohesive, with each item complimenting others, allowing for easy mixing and matching. By focusing on timeless styles rather than fleeting trends, a time capsule wardrobe promotes sustainability and a more conscious approach to fashion.

I have myself never gone with the trends in the fashion industry, I call them fads because they keep changing all the time. Keeping up with so many changes for people who do not have much idea about styling is not easy. This is why a time capsule wardrobe makes it easy to go about your life with a support to build upon.

And as I said in the last chapter, I first start with the hair color, then eyebrows, lens, basic clothing, color palette, make up, and last but most importantly lingerie. As I would say, if the inner being is uncomfortable the outer look will never hold up. :)

Hair

Ever notice how a change in hairstyle or a good hair day can alter your mood? This signifies the importance that hair hold in making or breaking a look.

Hair is like the crown of your personality and it carries a lot of weightage in your entire look. Whether it's a carefree messy bun, sleek straight locks, or vibrant curls, your hair communicates a message about who you are and what you're about. It's a canvas for self-expression. This is why I always start here. A good haircut can enhance your facial features. The right hairstyle and hair color can make you look younger, better and prettier. A haircut that compliments your features can enhance your look manifold times.

Your hair frames your face. The better hairstyle you select, the more stylish you get. There are many purposes of cutting and styling hair. Keeping your hair healthy is also important.

A good hairstyle can make you look younger. Your hairstyle could actually take years off. On the other hand, the wrong haircut and hairstyle can make you look older.

Since hairstyle plays an important role in the way you look, I always suggest to my clients the hairstyle that matches their lifestyle. The hairstyle of working women should be different from high-school girls. Just like everything else, your hairstyle should reflect what you do.

Then, there are also some people who realize their true selves at some point of time in their lives and thus look for complete transformation. For such people also, starting with the hair is particularly important as the transformation must always start here. It adds so much confidence and vigor to start a new life, a new journey.

Eyebrows

The philosopher Pythagoras once defined beauty as nothing but symmetry. Human brains are wired to find solace and comfort in symmetry. They are wired to recognize patterns and order. Symmetry is a fundamental aspect of many patterns, and our brains tend to find symmetry visually appealing. If you look around, you'll find leaves, branches and flowers in absolute symmetry while also aligning in a way to leave spaces for beautiful new formations to take place. It is this that human beings are born to appreciate. Our faces also have symmetries and proportions and eyebrows hold great importance in the same.

Do you have a long face you want to volumize, a round face you want to slim, or maybe a hint of asymmetry you want to correct? The key lies with eyebrow shaping and finding a shape that compliments the facial features. Eyebrows can balance facial features, add length or roundness, minimize flaws, and help refine the final look by manipulating where the eye comes to rest on the face.

If the eyes are the windows to the soul, your eyebrows are the window dressings. And those brows can either be alluring, drawing attention in, or unpolished—ruining the whole look. When it comes to eyebrow shaping, the style is customized to your eye shape to best highlight this facial feature or hide any flaws that may exist.

Eye color

- Contrasting colors can make eyes stand out. Choosing clothing colors that contrast with the eye color can draw attention to the eyes and create a vibrant, striking effect. For instance, wearing warm tones like oranges or golds with cool-toned blue eyes can create a visually appealing contrast.

- Coordinating the overall color palette with eye color contributes to a cohesive and polished look. Harmonizing clothing colors with eye color can create a balanced and aesthetically pleasing ensemble. This doesn't necessarily mean matching the exact shade but choosing complementary tones.

- Eye color can be a reflection of one's personality and style preferences. Incorporating clothing colors that resonate with the individual's eye color can be a way to express their unique sense of style and create a look that feels authentic.
- Eye color is often linked to underlying skin tones. Taking both factors into account helps in selecting clothing colors that harmonize with the individual's overall complexion. This ensures that the chosen colors enhance the natural warmth or coolness of the skin.

Other aspects of clothing formula, makeup and color palette, I'll discuss in detail in the next chapter.

Note to aspiring stylists

Let's talk about why it's crucial for a stylist to work on themselves before transforming others. Picture this: you walk into a room, and without saying a word, people get a sense of who you are. That first impression is like 80% of the job for a stylist, and it's not just about skills; it's about how you carry yourself.

Think of that 80% as the vibe you give off, a mix of confidence, authenticity, and your personal style. It's what draws people in and makes them believe you can work magic with their look. Now, I'm not saying skills don't matter—they do, and that's the remaining 20%. But imagine having all the skills in the world without the confidence and style to back it up. It's like if you can’t cook good food, nobody will want to learn cooking from you for sure.

Your personal style isn't just about looking good; it's a way of communicating who you are without saying a word. It's the language that connects you with others. So, when you refine your own style, you're not just dressing up; you're opening up a conversation.

Think of the mirror as your canvas. How you present yourself is like the first brushstrokes of a painting. Work on perfecting those strokes because they set the stage for the 20% of skills you bring to the table. Your personal style is not an add-on; it's a crucial part of your toolkit.

So, remember that your style is not just about looking good—it's about making a connection. I got my first client because of this reason alone. I dressed my thoughts, my life, my personality through my clothes and the people whom I would meet, they would love my style. They wanted the same from me for themselves. And it’s how my style and my skill together worked out for me and for them.

CHAPTER 4

The dressing formula

1. **Dress according to your personality not mood:** You know the famous Mark Zuckerberg style right? He has probably 7 pairs of the same t-shirt in the same style and color. His attire represents his personality very well. Now, I am not saying that go as basic as him but what I am meaning to say is that your style is the character that you hold. Even when you are going through the fluctuations and the ups and downs in the mood, you can feel grounded when you have a particular sense of style to rely upon. If you work in the corporate you would definitely understand the value of this formula because if one day you don't feel alright, you can't just get up, wear something informal and go to your office. Your style is your character and should not change too much so as to create a confusion as to who you actually are. First understand who you are and then use that knowledge to curate a style that works for you. Contrary to popular belief fashion is not about change, it is about consistency. Actors and actresses change their look because they have to represent the different characters that they hold and accordingly change the style. But in real life, we don't change our characters that often, we evolve surely but the

core never changes. So, you dress according to your core, not the layers that keep changing.

2. **Formula of colors :** One of the most common mistakes that people make in curating an outfit is the color. They will mix and match fabrics but will forget to match the colors. Colors can be matched intuitively as well but a lot of other factors can influence the tone and the shade of a color, like the mirror, lighting, perception. Therefore, if you think you are not that great with color gradience, you can try this simple formula based on Color theory. Color theory in fashion refers to the study and application of colors in clothing and accessories to create visually appealing and harmonious outfits. This can come in most handy while buying clothes online, you can use the given name of the color and see if it matches items that are already there in your wardrobe or if it even matches your skin tone. So, color theory involves understanding how different colors interact with each other, how they can be combined to evoke specific emotions or moods, and how they can complement an individual's skin tone and personal style.

Color theory in fashion refers to the study and application of colors in clothing and accessories to create visually appealing and harmonious outfits. It involves understanding how different colors interact with each other, how they can be combined to evoke specific emotions or moods, and how they can complement an individual's skin tone and personal style.

☆ **Key components of color theory in fashion include:**

- **Color Wheel:** The color wheel is a circular diagram of colors arranged by their chromatic relationship. It typically includes primary colors (red, blue, and yellow), secondary colors (green, orange, and purple), and tertiary colors (a combination of a primary and a secondary color). The arrangement helps identify color relationships and schemes.

☆ **Primary, Secondary, and Tertiary Colors:**

- **Primary Colors:** Red, blue, and yellow are considered the foundation colors and cannot be created by mixing other colors.

- **Secondary Colors:** Green, orange, and purple are formed by mixing two primary colors.
- **Tertiary Colors:** Colors like red-orange, yellow-green, and blue-violet are created by combining a primary and a secondary color.

☆ **Color Schemes:**

- **Complementary Colors:** Colors opposite each other on the color wheel, such as red and green or blue and orange.
- **Analogous Colors:** Colors that are next to each other on the color wheel, creating a harmonious and cohesive look.
- **Triadic Colors:** Three colors evenly spaced around the color wheel, providing balance and contrast.

☆ **Warm and Cool Colors:**

- **Warm Colors:** Reds, oranges, yellows, and browns are considered warm colors and can evoke energy and vibrancy.
- **Cool Colors:** Blues, greens, purples, and grays are cool colors, often associated with calmness and serenity.

☆ **Color Temperature and Skin Tone:**

- Understanding the warmth or coolness of colors concerning an individual's skin tone.
- Choosing colors that complement and enhance the natural undertones of the skin.

☆ **Color Psychology:**

- The psychological impact of colors and how they can influence emotions and perceptions.
- Using color to convey specific messages or evoke particular feelings in fashion.

☆ **Application in Outfits:**

- Creating visually appealing outfits by combining colors strategically.
- Considering factors like color blocking, pattern mixing, and accessory choices to enhance the overall look.

Imagine that You have a classic navy blue blazer and want to create a sophisticated outfit with a pop of color.

Color Theory Application: Complementary Colors

1. **Dominant Color:** Navy Blue (Primary Color)

- Start with the navy blue blazer as the primary color, setting the tone for a classic and timeless look.

2. **Complementary Color:** Orange (Opposite on the Color Wheel)

- Choose orange as the complementary color to navy blue. This creates a bold and eye-catching contrast.

☆ **Outfit Details:**

- **Navy Blue Blazer (Primary Color):** Wear a tailored navy blue blazer as the foundation of your outfit. It adds sophistication and serves as a neutral base.

- **Crisp White Button-Up Shirt:** Pair the blazer with a crisp white button-up shirt for a clean and polished look. White complements both navy blue and orange.

- **Orange Skinny Pants:** Opt for a pair of slim-fit orange pants as the complementary color. The orange adds vibrancy and becomes the focal point of the outfit.

- **Brown Leather Belt:** Define the waist with a brown leather belt. Brown is a neutral color that complements both navy blue and orange.
- **Brown Loafers or Ankle Boots:** Complete the look with brown leather loafers or ankle boots. The brown footwear grounds the outfit and provides a cohesive transition between the navy blue and orange.
- **Gold Accessories:** Add gold accessories, such as a statement watch or earrings, to introduce a touch of elegance and tie in with the warm tones of orange.

Result:

By using complementary colors, you've created a visually striking outfit that balances the classic appeal of navy blue with the boldness of orange. The white shirt and brown accessories contribute to a well-rounded and harmonious look. This example demonstrates how color theory can guide your choices to achieve a cohesive and stylish outfit with a pop of color.

Example 2# You have a beautiful purple-colored kurti and want to create a warm, elegant look for a family function.

Dominant Color: Purple (Primary Color)

- The purple kurti remains the central and dominant color, embracing the comfort and richness of the hue.

☆ **Outfit Details:**

- **Purple Anarkali Kurti (Primary Color):** Choose a flowy and comfortable purple Anarkali kurti. Opt for breathable fabric to ensure ease during the family gathering.

- **Matching Churidar Pants:** Pair the kurti with matching purple churidar pants. The monochromatic combination creates a cohesive and soothing aesthetic.

- **Gold Jhumka Earrings:** Enhance the traditional touch with gold jhumka earrings. The gold complements the regality of the purple and adds a subtle ethnic flair.

- **Purple Dupatta with Gold Border (Optional):** If you wish to add a layer, drape a lightweight purple dupatta with a gold border over one shoulder. This adds a touch of grace without being overly formal.

- **Comfortable Mojari Shoes:** Opt for comfortable and embellished mojari shoes. The footwear combines tradition with comfort, allowing you to move freely during the family gathering.

- **Subtle Purple Bindis (Optional):** You may consider adding subtle purple bindis for a cultural touch. This small detail complements the overall color scheme without being too elaborate.

- **Simple Gold Bracelet:** Wear a simple gold bracelet to complement the earrings and add a hint of understated elegance.

RESULT:

The monochromatic comfortable look featuring the purple kurti is perfectly suited for a family function at home. The combination of purple with gold accents creates a warm look.

Creating fashionable and attention-grabbing outfits often involves experimenting with various fabrics. Mixing and matching textiles can elevate your fashion sense, adding depth and visual interest to your overall look. However, achieving the perfect balance when combining fabrics can be a bit tricky.

☆ Understand Fabric Types:

- To successfully mix and match fabrics, it's essential to have a good understanding of different fabric types and their characteristics. Familiarize yourself with fabrics such as cotton, silk, denim, chiffon, linen, wool, velvet, and more. Each fabric has its own texture, weight, drape, and sheen, influencing how they interact when combined.

☆ Consider Color and Pattern Coordination:

- Pay attention to color and pattern coordination when mixing fabrics. Aim for a cohesive and harmonious look by selecting fabrics that complement each other. Choose fabrics in similar or complementary colors, or opt for contrasting shades to make a bold statement. Mix patterns like florals, stripes, and checks, ensuring they share a common color or theme for visual coherence.

☆ Play with Textures:

- Texture is a key element in fabric mixing.

Combining different textures adds depth and tactile interest to your outfits. Mix smooth fabrics like silk or satin with textured materials such as tweed or lace. Experiment with combinations that create visual and tactile contrast, balancing matte and shiny surfaces, as well as soft and structured fabrics.

☆ **Balance Proportions:**

- Achieve a visually pleasing ensemble by balancing proportions when mixing fabrics. If you choose a voluminous fabric for one piece, balance it with a more fitted or streamlined fabric for another. For example, pair a flowy silk blouse with tailored trousers or a structured blazer with a lightweight chiffon skirt. Strive for a balanced silhouette that flatters your body shape.

☆ **Layering Techniques:**

- Experiment with layering different fabrics to add depth and dimension to your outfit. Layer lightweight fabrics over heavier ones or combine sheer fabrics with opaque materials. Play with lengths, allowing different fabric layers to strategically peek out. Accessories like scarves, belts, or vests can also be used for layering, enhancing your textile mix.

☆ **Pay Attention to Occasion and Season:**

- Consider the occasion and season when mixing fabrics. Opt for breathable and lightweight textiles during warmer months and reserve heavier fabrics for colder seasons. Choose elegant fabrics like silk or velvet for formal events and opt for denim or cotton blends for casual outings. Adapting fabric choices to the occasion and season ensures both comfort and style.

☆ **Trust Your Intuition and Experiment:**

- While guidelines are helpful, fashion is an art form that allows for creative expression. Trust your intuition and experiment with fabric mixing. Don't be afraid to break traditional fashion rules and try unexpected combinations. Innovative and stunning looks often emerge from daring textile mixtures. Have fun with your fashion choices and let your personal style shine.

CONCLUSION:

Mixing and matching fabrics is a delightful way to enhance your personal style and create unique outfits. By understanding fabric types, considering color and pattern coordination, playing with textures, balancing proportions, layering, and adapting to occasions, you can master the art of fabric mixing. Remember to trust your intuition and have fun with your fashion experiments. With these tips, you'll confidently step into a world of endless possibilities in women's textile combinations.

Example 1# Central Fabric : Wool Blend (Primary Element)

Opt for a well-tailored wool blend pencil skirt in a neutral tone for a sophisticated and professional touch.

☆ **Outfit Details:**

- **Silk Blouse (Primary Fabric):** Pair the pencil skirt with a silk blouse in a complementary color, adding a touch of luxury and refinement.

- **Structured Wool Blazer (Secondary Element):** Layer with a structured wool blazer, harmonizing with the skirt's fabric for a cohesive and polished look.

- **Closed-Toe Leather Heels:** Complete the ensemble with closed-toe leather heels, maintaining a professional and polished appearance.

- **Pearl Necklace:** Accentuate the neckline with a simple pearl necklace, offering a subtle and elegant accessory.

- **Leather Briefcase or Tote:** Carry a leather briefcase or tote to hold important documents, seamlessly integrating style with practicality.

- **Classic Watch:** Wear a classic watch for a functional and refined accessory that complements the overall professional attire.

- **Minimalistic Bracelet (Optional):** Optionally, add a minimalistic bracelet for a touch of personal style without being overly distracting.

RESULT:

This professional ensemble, centered around a wool blend pencil skirt, emphasizes the importance of fabric choices in creating a polished and sophisticated look for a business meeting. The combination of silk, wool, and leather ensures both comfort and elegance, contributing to an outfit that exudes confidence and professionalism.

Example 2# Party-Ready Fabric Mix and Match:

☆ **Central Fabric:** Velvet (Primary Element)

- Choose a luxurious velvet A-line midi skirt in a rich jewel tone like emerald green or deep burgundy as the focal point of your party outfit.

☆ **Outfit Details:**

- **Sequin Embellished Top (Secondary Element):** Pair the velvet skirt with a sequin embellished sleeveless top for a glamorous and eye-catching element.
- **Faux Fur Bolero or Stole:** Layer with a faux fur bolero or stole for added texture and a touch of sophistication, especially during

colder seasons.

- **Statement High Heels:** Complete the look with statement high heels featuring metallic accents or glitter for an extra dose of party glamour.
- **Dangling Statement Earrings:** Adorn dangling statement earrings that complement the sequins, adding sparkle to your overall ensemble.
- **Clutch with Metallic Details:** Carry a clutch with metallic details or sequin embellishments, tying together the elements of your outfit.
- **Stack of Bracelets (Optional):** Optionally, wear a stack of metallic or beaded bracelets for a playful and trendy touch.

Result:

This fabric mix and match for a party outfit combines the opulence of velvet with the sparkle of sequins, creating a visually stunning and festive ensemble. The addition of faux fur and metallic accents adds depth and texture, making it perfect for a celebratory occasion. The carefully chosen accessories enhance the overall glamorous and party-ready look.

3. Dress according to your body, skin tone and profession

Dress According to Your Body, Skin Tone, and Profession: Elevating Your Style

Understanding Your Body:

Dressing according to your body shape is a fundamental aspect of cultivating a stylish and flattering wardrobe. Every individual has unique body proportions, and choosing clothing that compliments these features can enhance your overall appearance. For instance, if you have an hourglass figure, emphasizing your waist with fitted styles can accentuate your natural curves. Alternatively, if your body shape is more rectangular, introducing layers and varied textures can create the illusion of curves. The key is to celebrate your body's distinct attributes and select garments that highlight your strengths while offering a comfortable and confident fit.

Harmonizing with Your Skin Tone:

Your skin tone plays a pivotal role in determining which colors complement and enhance your overall look. Identifying whether you have warm or cool undertones can guide your color choices effectively. If your undertones lean towards warm hues, earthy tones like oranges, yellows, and browns can be particularly flattering. On the other hand, cool undertones are complemented by cooler shades such as blues, purples, and greens. Understanding your skin tone ensures that the colors you wear harmonize with your complexion, creating a cohesive and polished appearance.

Professional Attire Aligned with Your Career:

Selecting clothing that aligns with your profession is a key element of projecting a polished and competent image in the workplace. Different industries have varying expectations regarding dress codes, ranging from formal business attire to more casual or creative styles. Tailoring your wardrobe to suit your professional environment not only showcases your awareness of workplace norms but also communicates a level of respect and commitment to your role. While creative professions may embrace bolder and trendier choices, more conservative fields often call for classic and understated pieces that convey professionalism and reliability.

In conclusion, dressing according to your body, skin tone, and profession involves a thoughtful and personalized approach to fashion. By celebrating your unique body shape, understanding your skin's undertones, and adhering to professional expectations, you can curate a wardrobe that not only looks good but also aligns seamlessly with your individuality and the demands of your career.

4. Formula for Matching patterns

Understanding the diverse range of colors, patterns, and fabrics in your wardrobe and learning how to harmonize them enables endless outfit possibilities. However, mastering this art requires practice and experimentation.

If you're unsure where to begin, this guide provides insights into the principles of mixing and matching patterns and offers valuable tips on achieving a well-dressed and sustainable appearance.

How to Combine Patterns Successfully:

(I). Simple Patterns

☆ Stripes:

One of the most recognized patterns, stripes come in various styles, including pinstripes, broad stripes, and diagonals. Pairing stripes with solid colors provides a balanced look. Trendspotter dubs stripes as the "neutral of prints," making them versatile and easy to pair with almost anything.

☆ Plaid (and Tartan):

Plaids feature two or more colors woven into horizontal and vertical bands. Bold and often bolder, plaids can be incorporated through accessories or paired with neutrals for a balanced appearance.

☆ **Checks (and Gingham):**

A checkered design resembles a chessboard with horizontal and vertical stripes. Gingham, a check pattern with bold color and white combinations, is a classic. Incorporate checks with a button-down shirt or accessories for a timeless look.

(II). ADVANCED PATTERNS

☆ **Herringbone:**

Common in suits, shirts, and accessories, herringbone gets its name from the fishbone-like weave pattern. Typically found in wool clothing, herringbone pieces like coats and blazers pair well with neutral colors for a sophisticated look.

☆ **Houndstooth:**

An alternative to traditional checks, houndstooth features broken corners, creating a diagonal appearance. This timeless pattern works well on shirts, accessories, and outerwear, offering versatility with both neutral and bright color pairings.

☆ **Paisley:**

Originating from Turkish and Middle Eastern design, paisley stands out with vibrant and contrasting colors. This bold pattern, with floral influences, can be found on various clothing items and accessories, making a striking fashion statement.

☆ **Polka Dots:**

Identical-sized circles form this classic pattern. Polka dots can be paired with solid colors for understated elegance or combined with other patterns like stripes, plaids, or florals for a bolder look.

☆ **Geometric Prints:**

Featuring shapes like triangles and squares, geometric prints can be abstract or detailed. These patterns shine best when allowed to be the focal point, with other clothing items kept understated and neutral.

☆ **Animal Prints:**

Inspired by spots, stripes, and scales found in

nature, animal prints make a bold statement. Start with animal print accessories if hesitant, gradually incorporating them into your wardrobe for a fierce and fashionable look.

Tips for Wearing Patterns:

☆ **Exercise Caution with Multiple Patterns:**

Be mindful of the number of patterns worn simultaneously. Start with adding one pattern to stripes or polka dots, often considered neutrals.

☆ **Balance Patterns:**

Whether wearing one or multiple patterns, balance or scale them effectively. Pair smaller designs with larger patterns for contrast, and let one pattern be the main focal point.

☆ **Start Simple:**

If new to wearing patterns, begin with simple combinations. Layer a subdued pattern over a striped top or experiment with a subtle design paired with a more vibrant pattern.

☆ Finding Sustainable Patterns:

Identifying your favorite patterns streamlines the search for sustainable versions. Sustainable brands offer a plethora of patterns and styles, aligning with eco-friendly fashion choices. Experiment, have fun, and soon, combining patterns will become second nature, providing a new way to create stylish and sustainable outfit combinations.

5. Confidence is fashion

☆ Fashion as a Cause of Confidence:

Fashion plays a significant role in instilling confidence, acting as a catalyst for self-assurance. One key aspect is the expression of individuality through clothing choices. When individuals wear outfits that align with their personal style and preferences, they can authentically communicate who they are, contributing to a sense of confidence derived from self-expression.

Empowerment through style is another way in which fashion influences confidence. Certain clothing choices, such as donning outfits that make one feel empowered and in control, can impact mindset positively.

Positive body image is closely linked to fashion's impact on confidence. When individuals choose clothing that enhances their comfort and flatters their body, it contributes to a positive perception of their physical selves. Fashion becomes a tool for cultivating a healthy body image, fostering self-esteem. Attention to detail in grooming, styling, and outfit coordination is a subtle yet powerful way in which fashion influences confidence. The act of taking care in one's appearance and presenting oneself with thoughtfulness can translate into increased self-assuredness. Feeling put-together and polished can positively affect the way individuals carry themselves, reinforcing confidence.

☆ **Fashion as an Effect of Confidence:**

Confidence, as an internal quality, often manifests in outward expressions, including personal style and fashion choices. Confident individuals tend to make bolder style choices, experimenting with unique and distinctive fashion statements. Their confidence allows them to step outside traditional fashion norms, contributing to the creation of innovative and inspiring styles.

Comfort in personal style is a notable effect of confidence on fashion. Individuals who exude confidence are more likely to embrace their unique style without being swayed by external opinions. This comfort in personal style leads to the development of a distinct and recognizable fashion identity, influencing the larger fashion landscape.

The impact of confidence extends beyond personal style to trends within the fashion industry. Confident individuals, often recognized as trendsetters, have the ability to influence and shape fashion trends. Their willingness to embrace new styles and push boundaries can have a ripple effect, contributing to the evolution of fashion on a broader scale.

Furthermore, confident individuals serve as positive influencers within the fashion community. Their energy and self-assurance can inspire others to feel more confident about their own style choices. This positive influence contributes to a more diverse, inclusive, and empowering fashion landscape, where individuals are encouraged to embrace their uniqueness and express themselves confidently through clothing.

In conclusion, the relationship between fashion and confidence is dynamic and reciprocal. Fashion can act both as a cause and an effect of confidence, creating a symbiotic connection that influences self-perception, personal style, and the broader trends within the fashion community.

CHAPTER 5

Importance of lingerie

Lingerie hides beneath the layers of those fabulous outfits that you spend days crafting. Most of us don't even give it a thought as to what underwear would go with what outfits. It's considered more of something that is utilitarian rather than something that is actually part of an outfit or a look. This is why what goes inside a dress is not paid much attention to. A totally well crafted look can go drastically wrong, if it is not aligned with the right type of underwear.

What is the importance of lingerie?

There's nothing unusual about body insecurity, but unfortunately, it can prevent you from enjoying an intimate relationship with yourself and your partner. If you discover the right way to find lingerie that flatters your body, your curves, your femininity, not only can you shift your mindset from self-hatred to self love, but you can begin to grow comfortable in your own skin.See unlike other pieces of an outfit, lingerie is a very personal item. It tells you a lot about how much care you hold for your body and its beauty is for very intimate connections to be shown to. This is why it is considered as an act of self love and self care. Beyond going all philosophical about it, lingerie even technically holds a very important part in the fashion world.

Lingerie is the soul of the outfit, it is the support that keeps your body in alignment. As women our bust and our pelvis are the most delicate and intimate body parts, which require their own share of clothing. Just how shoes are important for your feet, innerwear is the sanctum of the intimate parts. Lingerie is the adaptive part of an outfit. It can take the form, tone, style and shape of whatever look you are trying to pull. However, this piece of clothing is compromised the most. You must have seen the ads that show men's underwear impacting their personalities and confidence significantly, well it is true but obviously not to the extent where it is shown that their underwear becomes the reason for magnetically attracting women. But surely the right fabric, fit and shape, does have a positive impact on a person's mood and confidence. In a U.S. nationwide poll by ShopSmart, 25 percent of self-identified women revealed that their moods were affected by "unattractive" or ill-fitting underwear.

They also discovered that almost half the women polled (47 percent), felt sexier or more confident when wearing a special pair of underwear.

The opposite is also true for an ill fitting underwear, that irritates the skin and ducks into places, affecting the person's mood and confidence negatively. Now, think about this, a peeking bra strap from a graceful black fitting dress would obviously not look so graceful. It would give an impression that the outfit is not brought together quite nicely. However, if you are wearing a white shirt and underneath you layer it with a complimenting bralette, that shows a little bit but aligns well with the style of the look, it totally changes the game. Therefore it is about thinking of your lingerie, your innerwear as part of your outfit and not just randomly matching anything with everything. I always say that you should invest and build a wardrobe that lasts for a longer period of time but the same is not true for lingerie. This goes by a different set of rules and these rules will help you to pull off any look you want without having to think about the discomfort on the inner side. I always suggest my clients to go with these basic rules while buying lingerie.

Rule No. 1: Going to a store every 6 month

- Going to a store to get your lingerie is the best way of going about it. We often do not understand how to take the right measurements and find the right garments that fit the size. This is where professional help comes in handy. You can go into the stores and get yourself measured to find the fit for yourself. Moreover our bodies undergo some morphological changes every six months, impacting parts of the body differently. The size of the bust and pelvis also changes accordingly, this is why you should frequent a store every six months to track the changes that these areas are undergoing. These changes can occur due to weight fluctuations, changes in fitness levels, or other factors. Regularly updating lingerie allows you to ensure that you have items that fit well and provide proper support.

Lingerie, especially bras and underwear, also can undergo wear and tear over time due to frequent washing and use. Replacing them every six months ensures that you have items in good condition.

- Fashion trends evolve, and personal style preferences may change. Just like how you buy new clothes every season, a six month cycle to buy lingeries also helps to incorporate new styles and designs into their wardrobe.
- Investing in new lingerie is a form of self-care. It's like caring for the inner you.
- There are so many cool types of lingerie, from lacy bralettes to fancier corsets. When you decide to buy, it's not just about getting underwear; it's like picking out clothes that make you feel awesome.

Rule No. 2: Go for the Nudes and the Blacks:

We all love a wardrobe full of colors but.... A time capsule for lingerie is built around two main colors, nudes and blacks.

Nudes and blacks are classic and versatile

colors in lingerie, and their importance lies in their ability to cater to diverse preferences, complement various skin tones, and serve different purposes in the world of intimate apparel.

- Nudes and blacks are neutral colors that seamlessly blend with different outfits, making them versatile choices for everyday wear. These colors are less likely to show through light-colored or sheer clothing, providing a discreet and polished appearance.
- Nudes, in particular, are chosen for their ability to match a range of skin tones. The primary purpose of nude bras is to create a seamless and natural look under clothing, and matching the color closely to your skin tone contributes to this effect. Selecting a nude bra that matches your skin tone is very important to ensure a seamless and natural look. Begin by identifying your skin undertone—whether it's warm (yellow or peachy tones), cool (pink or blue tones), or neutral. This will guide you in choosing a nude shade that harmonizes with your skin. Pay attention to the depth of your skin tone, selecting a shade that closely resembles your

natural coloring. Many lingerie brands offer a variety of nude options to cater to different skin tones. When shopping, consider trying on bras under different lighting to gauge how well the color blends with your skin. Additionally, consulting with fitting experts or using online tools provided by lingerie brands can assist you in finding the perfect match. Ultimately, the goal is to achieve a discreet and polished appearance, where the nude bra seamlessly blends with your skin tone, creating an invisible foundation for various outfits and occasions.Lingerie in nude shades can create a flattering and natural look, offering a subtle, second-skin effect that enhances the overall aesthetic. Blacks, while not skin-toned, are known to flatter all skin tones and are associated with power.

- Black lingerie is also associated with sophistication and timeless elegance. It has a classic appeal that transcends trends, making it a popular choice for special occasions or when someone wants to feel effortlessly chic and alluring.
- Both nude and black lingerie have the

potential to enhance body confidence. Nude lingerie can create a seamless silhouette, while black lingerie can highlight and flatter curves, providing a sense of empowerment and allure.

- These colors are less likely to go out of style, ensuring that investment in these pieces of can provide long-term value.
- Nudes and blacks can effortlessly adapt to changing fashion trends. Whether someone prefers a classic and understated look or desires to incorporate trendy designs into their lingerie collection, these colors can serve as a neutral canvas for various styles.
- Nudes and blacks are considered wardrobe staples in lingerie, forming the foundation of a well-rounded collection. These colors can serve as the base for layering with other colors or more elaborate pieces, allowing for mixing-and-matching.

Rule No. 3: Choosing right strap and support

The primary importance of choosing the right bra strap and support lies in comfort. Ill-fitting or unsupportive bras can lead to discomfort, irritation, and even pain. The right straps and support ensure that the bra provides proper coverage and fits snugly without digging into the skin.

A bra with adequate support is also essential for maintaining good posture and back health. Bras that lack proper support often are one of the biggest reasons that lead to back and shoulder pain, especially for women with larger bust sizes. The right bra straps distribute weight evenly, reducing strain on the shoulders and upper back.

Most people think that the main bust support in a bra comes from the strap around the shoulders. However, in reality the main support comes from the strap that wraps around your under bust. This strap should neither be too tight or too loose. Some women think that if they buy a smaller size, their figure might slim down but this causes extra fat to bulge out of the strap, making it look ungraceful and causing discomfort. Choose a bra that has a wider strap for the underbust as it provides more support. A well-fitted bra with appropriate support helps maintain the shape and integrity of the breasts. The right support minimizes bouncing and movement, which is particularly important during physical activities.

Similarly when it comes to straps around the shoulders, their main function is to hold the bra in the position around the bust. For people who have heavier busts, they can go with wider straps and for normal bust sizes, experimenting with the strap width is acceptable.

Rule No. 4: The right size matters

When you read the bra size that says 32B, it means that the underbust measure is 32 inches and B is actually the cup size, which is determined by the most wide part of the bust area. The size should first fit well to your underbust and then to the cup, this is what actually is the right fit. Supportive bras play a role in preventing breast sagging over time. The right bra straps and structure help lift the breasts, providing necessary support to the delicate breast tissues and ligaments.

Choosing a bra with the right support enhances the overall appearance of clothing. Well-supported breasts create a smoother silhouette, allowing clothing to drape more elegantly and improving the fit of outfits.

Wearing a bra that offers proper support can boost confidence. When women feel comfortable and well-supported, it positively influences their posture and self-assurance. This confidence can extend to various aspects of life.

Rule No. 5: Choose right Shapewears

Now there are occasions when you would want to wear sheer fabrics, light-colored garments, or outfits with a snug fit, where visible lines or bulges may be a concern.

This is where shapewears come in handy. The seamless and discrete nature of shapewear ensures that it remains invisible under clothing. Shapewear is a versatile styling tool that addresses a range of fashion needs, from creating a smooth silhouette to enhancing the fit of clothing.

☆ **Do's of Wearing Shapewear:**

- Do select shapewear in your correct size.

Wearing shapewear that is too tight can be uncomfortable and may create bulges rather than smooth lines.

- Do match the type of shapewear to your outfit. Different styles cater to various clothing types, so consider the neckline, hemline, and overall design of your outfit.

- Do step into shapewear or pull it up gradually to ensure it fits evenly. Avoid rolling it down or forcing it on, as this may compromise the effectiveness and comfort.

- Do try different styles of shapewear to find what works best for your body and outfit. Bodysuits, high-waisted shorts, and shaping tanks offer different levels of support and coverage.

- Do choose shapewear made from breathable fabrics, especially if you plan to wear it for an extended period. Fabrics with moisture-wicking properties can enhance comfort.

☆ **Don'ts of Wearing Shapewear:**

- Don't choose shapewear that is significantly smaller than your actual size. Sizing down excessively can lead to discomfort, difficulty breathing, and an uneven appearance.

- Don't wear shapewear with visible lines under tight-fitting clothing.
- Avoid shapewear that creates indentations or bulges under clothing, especially in areas like the waist, thighs, or bust.
- Don't wear shapewear under clothes that are too tight or ill-fitting. It may create unnecessary pressure points and discomfort.
- Don't choose shapewear in contrasting colors to your outfit. While nude shades are versatile, bold or contrasting colors may be visible under sheer or light-colored fabrics.
- Don't ignore the neckline compatibility between your shapewear and outfit. The wrong neckline can be visible or clash with the design of your dress or top.

Rule No. 6: Never buy online

While buying lingerie online is convenient and there are so many options that lucrate our eyes, it's essential to know that shoes and underwear should never be bought online.

- One of the primary reasons is the uncertainty about fit and sizing. Lingerie often requires precise measurements, and sizes can vary across brands and styles. Without trying items on before purchase, there's a high chance that the lingerie might not fit as expected.

- Lingerie is a sensory experience, and buying online eliminates the opportunity to assess the garment in person. You can't feel and assess the fabric and texture of lingerie items. Since comfort is crucial in intimate apparel, not being able to touch and examine the materials beforehand takes suitability and personalization out of the picture.

- The color representation on screens may have been enhanced and it might not reflect the actual color of the piece. This can actually be a headache when you are buying shades like nudes that match your skin tone.

- In physical stores, customers often benefit from the assistance of sales professionals who can provide guidance on styles, sizing, and fit. Online shopping lacks the in-person support that some individuals may find helpful, especially when choosing lingerie.

Rule No 7: Don't shy away

In the evolving landscape of fashion and personal expression, lingerie and sexy underwear have undergone a significant transformation from being exclusively associated with pleasing a partner to becoming a tool of self-empowerment. As psychologist Danielle Forshee rightly points out, there has been a historical perspective that lingerie is primarily for the benefit of a partner, often linked to societal expectations and traditional gender roles. However, contemporary women are rewriting this narrative, embracing a mindset that emphasizes self-love, confidence, and personal satisfaction.

In today's era of empowerment, women are taking ownership of their choices, asserting that lingerie is not solely for the pleasure or gaze of someone else but can be a source of joy and confidence for themselves. This shift in perspective represents a broader cultural movement where women are reclaiming their bodies, desires, and self-image. The act of choosing and wearing lingerie becomes a personal celebration, a form of self-expression that goes beyond external perceptions.

This shift is a reflection of the ongoing dialogue about body positivity, self-love, and breaking free from traditional norms. Women are embracing the idea that they can wear lingerie whenever they please, not dictated by societal expectations or a need to conform to traditional roles. It's about expressing their sensuality and style on their terms, fostering a sense of autonomy and confidence that transcends external validation.

In essence, this transformation in the perception of lingerie signifies a larger cultural movement where women are asserting their agency, challenging stereotypes, and celebrating their bodies in ways that make them feel confident and beautiful—regardless of external expectations. It's a powerful acknowledgment that personal empowerment and self-love are not contingent on others' opinions but are intrinsic and accessible at any time, with or without an audience.

You can specifically select lingerie that disguises problem areas, while putting your best features on display. The moment you slip into these carefully selected pieces, you'll feel proud of your body. This pride will immediately be evident to your significant other, who finds body confidence sexy. Stepping out of one's comfort zone often leads to personal growth and newfound confidence. Lingerie, with its alluring and sometimes daring nature, provides a subtle yet impactful way to embrace this philosophy. For those who typically avoid risks, venturing into the realm of lingerie can be an invigorating challenge. Unlike more drastic moves, exploring lingerie allows individuals to push boundaries in a manageable and personal way. The act of selecting and wearing lingerie can be a journey of self-discovery, encouraging a positive shift in self-perception and body confidence. The subtle yet transformative nature of lingerie allows individuals to express their sensuality and style, fostering a sense of empowerment. Ultimately, the decision to embrace lingerie is not just about the garments themselves but about the journey toward embracing one's own unique beauty and embracing new experiences. Stepping into the world of lingerie is a step towards broadening horizons, enhancing self-esteem, and celebrating the diverse facets of personal expression.

CHAPTER 6

Footwear

You must have come across this statement, "if you want to know a person, just look at what they are wearing on their feet". Just as we talked about lingerie, we must discuss the case of footwear as well. Both lingerie and footwear should never be bought online. You need to feel the fabric and also the comfort of the shoes, you don't wear a piece of footwear because it looks cute, you wear it because it is both beautiful and comfortable.

Today there is a constant push for sustainable fashion and footwear offers a big space to dive right into it. Go for quality over quantity. Have a few quality pairs of shoes that mesh well with your time capsule wardrobe and voila, you won't have to worry about matching elaborate prints on your footwear with the patterns on your clothes each time.

Footwear is the last item that we wear while heading out. But just because they are sequenced last, does it mean footwear can be compromised with? Absolutely No.

Footwear holds significant importance in almost every outfit, whether we consciously acknowledge it or not. While mismatched accessories, undershirts, and socks may go unnoticed, the same is not true for your footwear. Shoes are often the initial focal point that captures attention. Cinderella's prince found her because of the glass sandal and if it wasn't for her shoes, she would have never been found. I'm not implying that you'll find your prince because of your footwear but that is how important your feet and its coveralls are. In numerous situations, a poorly chosen shoe combination can easily overshadow the rest of the outfit, leaving little room for redemption in terms of overall appearance.

It might be astonishing how significantly your choice of shoes can impact the overall appearance of your outfit, especially for those who may not prioritize personal fashion. While some individuals accumulate more shoe pairs than outfits, others stick to a limited selection, perhaps even just a single pair, using them for various occasions. Even if you don't perceive any issues, it's essential to recognize that others might. Taking a moment to try on different pairs of shoes in front of a mirror can provide valuable insights into how they complement or alter your overall look.

But remember that marketing gimmicks will always try to sell you more and they do not care if you find the right thing or not. This is why you should go with building time capsules in footwears as well. Don't go after everything that is trending, that confusion and constant change will create chaos in your wardrobe. There are a few things that one should consider before buying or aligning a particular footwear item with the outfit. The rules remain somewhat similar to the ones that I had outlined for lingerie shopping.

Rule No. 1: Check Sizing Regularly

- Opting to visit a shoe store is the most effective way to ensure you find the right pair. Many individuals struggle with understanding how to accurately measure their feet and select shoes that perfectly match their size. This is where seeking professional assistance becomes invaluable. By visiting a store, you can have your feet measured to discover the ideal fit. Additionally, our feet can undergo changes due to factors like age, weight fluctuations, or other influences.

- Additionally, over time, shoes also undergo wear and tear, affecting their comfort and durability. Updating your footwear regularly is essential to ensure you have well-fitting shoes that offer proper support. Investing in good footwear is a form of self-care, a way of nurturing your overall well-being. There is a wide array of stylish footwear options, from casual sneakers to elegant heels. Choosing shoes goes beyond acquiring a piece of fashion, it's about selecting pairs that make you feel comfortable and confident with every step.
- Remember Monica from Friends Show? She had bought a pair of fancy black leather boots costing her money equivalent to her apartment's monthly rent. Although she advocated that these boots matches every outfit of hers but they were so uncomfortable that the entire money went to waste as she could not wear them without having her "feet bleed to death"(metaphorically).

Rule No. 2: Buying nudes and the blacks:

While we all cherish a wardrobe bursting with colors, the time capsule for footwear is anchored in two fundamental hues: nudes and blacks.

Nudes and blacks stand as timeless and adaptable colors in footwear, their significance lying in their capacity to cater to diverse preferences, complement various outfits, and serve distinct roles.

These neutral tones effortlessly blend with different ensembles, making them versatile choices for everyday wear. Their subdued nature makes them less likely to be visible through light-colored or sheer clothing, imparting a discreet and polished appearance.

Nude footwear, in particular, is chosen for its ability to harmonize with a spectrum of skin tones. The primary goal of nude shoes is to create a seamless and natural look, and selecting a shade that closely aligns with your skin tone is crucial. Determining your skin undertone, be it warm, cool, or neutral, guides you in choosing the right nude shade. Pay attention to the depth of your skin tone when selecting a hue that closely mimics your natural coloring. Many footwear brands offer a variety of nude options to cater to different skin tones. When shopping, try on shoes under different lighting to gauge how well the color blends with your skin. Consulting with fitting experts can also assist you in finding the perfect match. The ultimate aim is to achieve a discreet and polished appearance where the nude footwear seamlessly blends with your skin tone, creating an invisible foundation for various outfits and occasions. Shoes in nude shades can create a flattering and natural look, offering a subtle, second-skin effect that enhances the overall aesthetic.

On the other hand, black footwear, while not skin-toned, is known to flatter all outfits and is associated with sophistication and timeless elegance. Its classic appeal transcends trends, making it a popular choice for special occasions or when someone wants to feel effortlessly chic and alluring.

Both nude and black footwear have the potential to enhance overall confidence. Nude shoes can create a seamless silhouette, while black footwear can add a touch of power and flatter various ensembles, providing a sense of empowerment.

These colors are less likely to go out of style, ensuring that investing in these pieces can provide long-term value. Nudes and blacks can effortlessly adapt to changing fashion trends, serving as a neutral canvas for various styles, whether one prefers a classic and understated look or desires to incorporate trendy designs into their footwear collection.

Considered wardrobe staples in footwear, nudes and blacks form the foundation of a well-rounded collection, serving as a base for layering with other colors or more elaborate pieces, allowing for versatile mixing and matching.

Rule No. 3: Choosing right strap and support

Footwear with appropriate support is crucial for maintaining good foot health and posture. Shoes lacking proper support are often a leading cause of foot pain, especially for individuals who spend extended periods on their feet or have specific foot conditions. The right shoe support helps distribute weight evenly, reducing strain on the feet, ankles, and lower back.

While many believe that the primary support in footwear comes from the sole and arch support, in reality, the main support comes from the structure around the instep. This part of the shoe should neither be too tight nor too loose. Some individuals might think that opting for a smaller size will make their feet appear smaller, but this can lead to discomfort and may cause the feet to spill over the sides. Choosing shoes with a wider structure around the instep provides more support and comfort.

Similarly, when it comes to straps or closures in footwear, their primary function is to hold the shoe in place around the foot. For those with wider or heavier feet, opting for wider straps or closures can provide additional support and prevent discomfort. Individuals with standard foot sizes have the flexibility to experiment with strap width based on personal preferences and style choices.

Rule No. 4: The right size matters

The right size will support your feet to be in shape, avoid injuries or foot conditions. Just take care of finding what pair fits you the most and gives you the most comfort.

Rule No. 5: Never buy online

While purchasing footwear online offers convenience and a plethora of tempting options, it's crucial to note that shoes, much like underwear, should never be bought online.

One of the primary concerns revolves around the uncertainty of fit and sizing. Footwear demands precise measurements, and sizes can fluctuate across brands and styles. Without the opportunity to try on shoes before making a purchase, there's a significant risk that the shoes may not fit as expected.

Footwear is an experience of the touch, and online shopping eliminates the chance to physically assess the fabric, quality and comfort of your footwear. The inability to feel and examine the fabric, texture, and overall construction takes away the crucial elements of suitability and personalization.

The representation of colors on screens may be manipulated, leading to discrepancies between the displayed and actual colors of the shoes. This becomes particularly problematic when selecting shades that need to match your skin tone, specific preferences or outfits.

In physical stores, customers often benefit from the assistance of knowledgeable sales professionals as well, who can offer guidance on styles, sizing, and fit. The absence of in-person support in online shoe shopping may pose challenges for individuals seeking expert advice to make informed choices about their footwear.

CHAPTER 7

The Indian influence

India in itself is a land of diversity. So many different cultures have found a home for themselves in the rich land of India. Our modern styles take a lot of influence from the past and even if we call ourselves the children of contemporary couture, our fashion has some parts rooted in our culture.

Indian fashion has a rich and diverse evolution deeply rooted in its cultural heritage. Historically, clothing in India has been shaped by a myriad of cultural influences, reflecting the country's diverse regions, communities, and historical interactions. Traditional garments like sarees, dhotis, and turbans were not just clothing items but symbolic expressions of regional identities and cultural nuances. Traditional garments like the saree, worn in various draping styles across regions, showcase the diverse cultural influences. For instance, the Kanjeevaram silk saree from South India and the Banarasi silk saree from North India exhibit the traditional craftsmanship and regional aesthetics.

The Mughal era marked a significant chapter in the evolution of Indian fashion. The fusion of

Persian and Indian styles led to the emergence of regal attire, characterized by intricate embroidery, luxurious fabrics, and flowing silhouettes. This era introduced a level of opulence that influenced both courtly and everyday fashion, leaving an indelible mark on traditional Indian garments. The Mughal influence is evident in the Anarkali suit, characterized by its flowing silhouette and intricate embroidery. This fusion of Persian and Indian styles is embodied in garments that blend regal Mughal aesthetics with traditional Indian craftsmanship.

The British colonial rule in India brought about a distinctive blend of Western and Indian fashion. Traditional attire coexisted with Victorian influences, leading to a fusion that combined the elegance of Indian textiles with Western cuts and styles. The saree continued to be a symbol of grace, while men's clothing saw the adoption of Western suits. This period of cultural exchange laid the foundation for a unique sartorial landscape. During the British colonial period, the adaptation of Western suits for men and the coexistence of Victorian-influenced blouses with traditional sarees exemplify the fusion of Indian and Western styles. The clothing choices during this period reflect the cultural amalgamation.

Post-independence, there was a resurgence of interest in traditional Indian textiles and craftsmanship. Designers and artisans sought to revive ancient weaving techniques, embroidery styles, and dyeing methods. The handloom movement gained momentum, emphasizing the beauty of handcrafted textiles and promoting sustainable practices. Traditional fabrics like Khadi became symbols of India's quest for self-sufficiency and cultural pride. The post-independence era witnessed the revival of traditional handloom fabrics. Khadi, promoted by Mahatma Gandhi, became a symbol of self-sufficiency and cultural pride. Handwoven textiles like Pochampally ikat and Phulkari embroidery saw a resurgence.

With the advent of globalization, Indian fashion experienced a dynamic shift. The influence of Western fashion and the rise of the Bollywood industry played an important role in shaping contemporary styles. Indian designers began experimenting with fusion wear, blending traditional elements with modern cuts and fabrics. The runway became a canvas for creativity, showcasing the diversity and adaptability of Indian fashion. The influence of Western fashion became visible in the popularity of Indo-Western fusion wear. An example is the fusion of a traditional Anarkali silhouette with contemporary cuts, creating a style that resonates with both Indian and global fashion preferences.

Marking a departure from well established dynastic influences, India's fashion evolution became intricately tied to its regional diversity. Each state started promoting its unique traditional attire, influenced by local customs, climate, and historical factors. A certain pride has started to emerge in the local roots causing the revival of ethnic wear, including intricate weaves, traditional embroidery, and indigenous fabrics. A inspiration from regional aesthetics, contributing to the celebration of India's cultural mosaic. The resurgence of regional textiles is exemplified by the popularity of Bandhani from Gujarat, known for its tie and dye technique. The contemporary adaptation of Bandhani patterns in modern clothing showcases the revival of traditional techniques.

In recent years, there also has been a growing emphasis on sustainable fashion and the preservation of cultural heritage. Designers are increasingly exploring eco-friendly practices, promoting handmade textiles, and collaborating with local artisans. This shift reflects a conscious effort to blend contemporary fashion with a commitment to preserving India's rich cultural legacy. The emphasis on sustainable fashion is reflected in the resurgence of Khadi as a symbol of eco-friendly and handmade textiles. Designers collaborating with local artisans to promote traditional crafts, like Ajrakh printing from Kutch, demonstrate a commitment to cultural preservation.

Indian textiles were also noted for their brilliant colors and prints. Besides that, traditional motifs, intricate embroidery, and unique dyeing methods showcased the diversity of India's cultural landscape. Each textile told a story or represented a specific region's traditions.

20 of the most iconic pieces from our past

☆ Saree:

- **Iconic Representation:** The saree is undoubtedly one of the most iconic and timeless pieces of Indian attire. Its history spans centuries, and it continues to be a symbol of grace, elegance, and cultural heritage.

☆ Sherwani:

- **Regal Attire:** The sherwani, with its origins in Mughal fashion, is a regal piece worn by men during weddings and special occasions. Its intricate embroidery and tailored silhouette make it a symbol of traditional Indian masculinity.

☆ Khadi:

- **Symbol of Independence:** Khadi, popularized by Mahatma Gandhi during the Indian independence movement, represents self-sufficiency and the spirit of the nation. The hand-spun and handwoven fabric is woven into various garments, emphasizing simplicity and sustainability.

☆ **Anarkali Suit:**

- **Mughal Elegance:** The Anarkali suit, inspired by the legendary dancer Anarkali in Mughal history, is a flowing, floor-length ensemble. Its graceful silhouette and intricate embroidery capture the timeless elegance of Mughal-inspired fashion.

☆ **Bandhani Saree:**

- **Tie and Dye Tradition:** The Bandhani saree from Gujarat is known for its vibrant colors and intricate tie and dye technique. It represents the rich textile heritage of the region and is often worn during festivals and celebrations.

☆ **Pheran:**

- **Kashmiri Heritage:** The Pheran is a traditional Kashmiri garment worn by both men and women. Its loose fit, intricate embroidery, and unique style make it a cultural symbol, especially during the winter months.

☆ **Turban (Safa):**

- **Cultural Headgear:** The turban, or safa, is

a traditional headgear worn by men across various regions in India. It holds cultural significance, indicating social status, religious beliefs, and regional identity.

☆ **Bindi:**

- **Symbolic Adornment:** The bindi, a decorative dot worn on the forehead, has deep cultural and spiritual significance. It is a symbol of auspiciousness, spirituality, and femininity, and is often worn during religious ceremonies and festivals.

☆ **Dhoti:**

- **Traditional Draping:** The dhoti is a traditional garment worn by men, especially in South India. Its simplicity and ease of draping make it a timeless piece, representing traditional attire that has stood the test of time.

☆ **Jodhpuri Pants:**

- **Equestrian Elegance:** Inspired by the equestrian heritage of Rajasthan, Jodhpuri pants are characterized by their unique cut and style. They have become a contemporary fashion statement, blending traditional elements with modern flair.

☆ **Lehenga Choli:**

- **Bridal Elegance:** The Lehenga Choli is a traditional three-piece ensemble worn by women, particularly during weddings and festivals. Its elaborate design, intricate embroidery, and vibrant colors make it an iconic choice for bridal wear.

☆ **Sherwani with Pagdi:**

- **Wedding Ensemble:** The combination of a Sherwani with a traditional Pagdi (turban) is a quintessential wedding attire for Indian grooms. The coordinated ensemble exudes regality and captures the essence of traditional Indian weddings.

☆ **Ghagra Choli with Odhni:**

- **Festive Splendor:** The Ghagra Choli, paired with an Odhni (dupatta), is a traditional attire worn by women during festivals and celebrations. The flowing skirt, embellished blouse, and draped dupatta create a captivating and festive look.

☆ **Patola Saree:**

- **Double Ikat Mastery:** The Patola saree from Gujarat is known for its intricate double ikat weaving technique. Each saree is a masterpiece, with vibrant geometric patterns, making it a symbol of exquisite craftsmanship and cultural heritage.

☆ **Nauvari Saree:**

- **Maharashtrian Tradition:** The Nauvari saree, draped in a distinctive nine-yard style, is a traditional Maharashtrian attire. It reflects the cultural richness of Maharashtra and is often worn during festivals, especially by Lavani dancers.

☆ **Mysore Silk Saree:**

- **Southern Splendor:** The Mysore Silk Saree is a luxurious silk drape from Karnataka known for its fine silk, vibrant colors, and intricate zari borders. It is a symbol of southern craftsmanship and is often worn during special occasions.

☆ **Phulkari Dupatta:**

- **Punjabi Embroidery:** The Phulkari dupatta, adorned with vibrant floral embroidery from Punjab, adds a burst of color to traditional attire. It is a symbol of Punjabi culture and is worn with pride during celebrations.

☆ **Patiala Salwar:**

- **Punjabi Comfort:** The Patiala Salwar, characterized by its loose and pleated design, originated in Punjab. Paired with a short kurta, it represents comfort and cultural identity, especially in North India.

☆ **Kanchipuram Silk Saree:**

- **Silken Opulence:** The Kanchipuram Silk Saree from Tamil Nadu is renowned for its luxurious silk, rich zari work, and vibrant color combinations. It is a staple for South Indian brides, symbolizing opulence and tradition.

☆ **Banarasi Brocade:**

- **Varanasi Elegance:** Banarasi brocade, originating from Varanasi, is known for its intricate gold and silver zari work. The

Banarasi saree, in particular, is a symbol of timeless elegance and is often passed down through generations.

CHAPTER 8

Navigating Personal Style

When it comes to my personal style, I have spent not days, not months, but years understanding and inculcating what represents me the best. My style revolves around mystery but I build that with ease. Mystery bears the curtain to the power that resides within and with my style I keep the prowess subtle and effortless. Even for my personal style I have kept the rules and the formulas the same.

Starting with the choice of colors, I find warm color tones to be my go-to palette. It compliments my skin tone, creating a radiant effect. I normally steer clear of cool tones, as they wash away the warmth from the face. Wearing cool shades on warm skin tones can sometimes create a contrast that may not be as flattering for some individuals. It has the potential to make the skin appear dull or sallow, and the colors may not harmonize well with the natural warmth of the complexion. My style is fundamentally basic, with a dash of statement pieces to add flair and individuality.

When it comes to patterns, simplicity rules the game for me. I opt for breathable fabrics, ensuring comfort without compromising style. Silhouettes play a crucial role, and I lean towards baggy fits. The voluminous look exudes a sense of power, especially when paired with pumps and textured fabrics.

Ethnic elements have always been a constant in my fashion choices, seamlessly blending with power dressing. Even in the corporate realm, I infuse a touch of ethnicity, making a distinctive statement. The key is standing out, and for me, that means incorporating ethnic touches into various styles.

I usually prefer to go less on accessories as I adhere to the rule of three, always adding a third layer to complete my look. Women often style a pair of jeans with a simple t-shirt but they forget to add the third layer. And for me this is the space that I use to create mystery and uniqueness in my outfit. Whether it's a summer blazer, a winter jacket, or a unique accessory like a hat or scarf, the third layer elevates the outfit and helps me stand out.

Your signature accessories, hats and nose pins,

embody a captivating duality that mirrors the richness of your personality. And as my very own signature additions, hats and nose pins are my top drawer selections. These two pieces hold a very special place in my overall ensemble, exuding a powerful vibe. Also the influence of culture has always been big on my life. And I symbolize this with adding nose pins to the game. I believe that nose pins introduce an ethnic charm and a nod to cultural diversity. I can wear a totally western outfit and add a dash of royalty to it with the quirk of a nose pin. It's like breaking the rules in a way that doesn't disturb the harmony of things but still puts the point across. And even so, I have always loved to bring together two different worlds that supposedly don't really belong together.

Walking in those high heels was my dream since childhood and even today, I can't get enough of the stilettos and pumps that dominate my collection. They are great at adding a touch of power to my stride and their sound reminds the little girl inside me that we made it.

Although Heels, pumps, stilettos are my forever

love, yet, I find balance by occasionally opting for Punjabi juttis as well, grounding myself back to the past and culture that I have come from. Punjabi juttis are works of art and today there are so many styles and options to choose from. Plus they are so comfortable as well. So, other than my usual heel love, Punjabi juttis are something that you'll find me wearing.

Lastly you'll find me experimenting a lot with Jackets. They are a focal point of my fashion strategy. Whether it's a perfectly tailored blazer or a loose, baggy jacket with a unique signature, attention to detail is very important for me. I strict the color palette to neutrals; I embrace timelessness with the old good leather jackets and adorn the new funk modern style with denim jackets being my constant favorite. They not only resonate with my style but also provide a versatile backdrop for my fashion expressions.

See, any creative field is not a day's job, it's like meditation, it takes years of understanding, peeling of layers to finally see the truth that hides within. And similarly, fashion is like that. Fashion is not shallow. It is a way of expressing the most hidden and true parts of yourself. My truest self belongs to the persona of a person who can contribute to bring smile, happiness and transformation in people's lives. Even today I live for that. I have gone through my share of struggles but the art that God has sent me with, it helped me survive through my bad share of life and I want to use the magic to help others as well. Fashion is a powerful tool. You can create so much with it. It's like painting and sculpting for your own self, you are the art and you are the artist. I believe it to be the most beautiful association between them. With years of my experience and understanding in inculcating the real identities with fashion, I have finally come to express my vision and my sense of style into my very own Label.

THE EXPRESSION OF THE FEMININE:

LABEL BHAVANA SINGH:

This has my heart, my soul and my life's work. My idea was always to celebrate the femininity of women. To showcase the feminine power through clothes and this is why Label Bhavana Singh speaks regal. The fashion that we represent takes you back to the days where femininity was royal. The designs we create are to empower the women of today. My label curates the idea that Indian women look the best when they feel the best and we believe that Indian women look the best in the regal ethnic attires. Indian women descend from the energies of beautiful, powerful, regal goddesses and they deserve to pool into the same rich heritage that has been part of our beloved and diverse country. We are in the modern age but we can bring our heritage to the times that we are present in and this is what our Label does.

Our ethnic wear has either been transformed to indo-western style or has only been limited to the special occasions of wedding functions, or other special occasions. But I want to bring the authentic cuts and designs back into the wardrobe of our modern women, reasserting the notion, old is gold. Regal is meant to be luxurious, the style of novelty. However, I believe that before the clothes that you wear, your mindset, your soul needs to feel the power that it is about to embody. Being a female is about embracing that inner goddess within you. It's not everyday that we get to reach out to that side of ours because of the way a normal routine functions. And seldom women forget that they are a form of the 'Shakti' that is responsible for running this world. This 'Shakti', this embodiment of a goddess is what is very subtly brought about by design pieces at the Label Bhavana Singh. It's what helps you reconnect with the power that is lying dormant within and trust me on this, clothes have an amazing way to do that. The way a silhouette touches the skin, the way a design falls upon your body, the colors that bring out the beauty in you, clothes do not just make you feel beautiful, the right ones can revive a part that you might have left somewhere behind in fulfilling the responsibilities as a "woman".

What is regal style?

Regal style refers to a fashion aesthetic that is characterized by elegance, sophistication, and a sense of grandeur. It draws inspiration from the clothing and accessories traditionally associated with royalty, nobility, and high societal status. Regal style often incorporates opulent fabrics, intricate detailing, and a focus on tailored and structured silhouettes. This fashion style exudes a sense of luxury and refinement, aiming to capture the timeless and majestic aura associated with royalty.

Regal style endeavors to evoke a majestic and grand aesthetic reminiscent of royalty. The aspiration is to capture a sense of opulence and luxury through the use of sumptuous fabrics like silk and velvet, along with elaborate embellishments and statement jewelry. The structured silhouettes and tailored fits inherent in regal fashion seek to convey authority and sophistication, reflecting a high societal status.

A central goal of regal style is to embrace timeless elegance, transcending fleeting trends by incorporating classic silhouettes, a sophisticated color palette, and meticulous attention to detail. Craftsmanship is celebrated, with a focus on intricate detailing, embroidery, and beading, highlighting the artistry and skill involved in creating luxurious pieces.

Drawing inspiration from historical periods associated with royalty, such as the Rajputana, different kingdoms, Mughal era, Victorian eras, regal style aims to capture a sense of heritage and tradition. The use of lehengas, dupattas, and dramatic outerwear contributes to a theatrical and dramatic presence, adding flair and ceremonial elegance to the overall look.

The intention is to convey a regal authority and make a statement. Individuals embracing regal style seek to establish a distinctive fashion identity by incorporating signature elements, whether through jewelry, accessories, or specific silhouettes.

Beyond the ephemeral nature of trends, regal style aspires to transcend the passage of time. By incorporating enduring elements and embracing a classic aesthetic, creating a lasting impression of timeless elegance and refined taste.

Key features of regal style include:

- **Rich Fabrics:** Regal style often utilizes luxurious fabrics such as silk, satin, velvet, and brocade. These materials contribute to a sense of opulence and richness in the overall look.

- **Intricate Detailing:** Attention to detail is crucial in regal style. Garments may feature intricate embroidery, embellishments, beadwork, lace, and other ornate elements that add a touch of extravagance.

- **Structured Silhouettes:** Regal fashion tends to favor structured and well-tailored silhouettes. This includes fitted bodices, A-line or ballgown skirts, and tailored suits that exude a sense of regal authority.

- **Jewelry and Accessories:** Accessories play a vital role in regal style. Statement jewelry, including tiaras, crowns, elaborate necklaces, and bejeweled earrings, contribute to the overall majestic appearance.

- **Classic Color Palette:** Regal style often features a classic and sophisticated color palette. Rich jewel tones such as deep reds, blues, emerald greens, and royal purples are commonly associated with regal fashion.

- **Capes and Cloaks:** Capes and cloaks are iconic elements of regal style, adding drama and flair to an outfit. They evoke a sense of authority and ceremonial elegance.

- **Elevated Outerwear:** Coats, jackets, and outerwear in regal style are often tailored and adorned with luxurious fur trims or embellishments, reflecting an elevated sense of fashion.

- **Haute Couture Influence:** Regal fashion often draws inspiration from haute couture, with an emphasis on craftsmanship, exclusivity, and the use of high-quality materials.

- **Formal and Eveningwear:** Regal style is particularly associated with formal and eveningwear. Ball gowns, evening dresses, and tailored suits for formal occasions embody the regal aesthetic.

- **Historical References:** Regal style may draw inspiration from historical periods associated with royalty, such as the Renaissance, Baroque, Rococo, or Victorian eras. Historical references contribute to the timeless and majestic feel.

Overall, regal style is about capturing a sense of

majesty and timeless elegance. It often transcends trends and embraces a classic, sophisticated aesthetic that reflects the grandeur and refinement traditionally associated with royalty and nobility.

MADHUBALA'S INFLUENCE:

When I was a kid, I would gather "pattis" (leftover pieces of cloth) and try to piece them together into little coveralls for pet birds and then I would sell them off to people. I can't remember a day when I didn't think of fabrics, clothes, designs, you should know by now that I have always been so into my craft. It's like you just know one thing in your life and it becomes almost equivalent to breathing, eating and it ultimately becomes your life. While I was growing up, her influence on me was like the possession of young Avni(Vidya Balan's character in Bhool Bhulaiya), by Manjulika. It wasn't just a fleeting interest; it became an integral part of my existence. Much like the way young Avni couldn't escape Manjulika's grip, Madhubala's timeless charm and cinematic legacy had a profound hold on my appreciation for art and style.Although I didn't dance like a lunatic on Ami je tomar, but,

I was inspired. Who was this fashion icon? Of course the magnanimous Madhubala. Her innocent face, big eyes, shoulder length natural curls and her confidence, everything about her was iconic. One of her boldest fashion statements included off-shoulder dresses in the 40s, a style that Madhubala carried with grace, making it a timeless trend still ruling the fashion game.

Madhubala defied norms by embracing hip wide trousers and checkered shirts, breaking away from the traditional Indian actress image which was just about saris and suits.

Her plain chiffon saris is one of the most iconic looks popularized by her.. Paired with heavy blouses, this trend is making a comeback even today, recalled by Alia Bhatt's saree wardrobe in the movie, Rocky and Rani.

She also pioneered buxom blouses, confidently pairing them with saris and skirts. With her curvy body and gorgeous face, Madhubala set a trend that has made a strong comeback in contemporary fashion.

Madhubala's unruly and wavy hair stood out in an era dominated by straight and curly hair trends, earning her the title of the 'out-of-bed look' trendsetter.

The iconic character she portrayed in "Anarkali" led to the everlasting popularity of Anarkali suits. Characterized by heavy long kurtas with extensive handwork, these suits continue to dominate the industry trends, proving Madhubala's lasting impact on Indian fashion.

Her influence still lasts on me. A child fan still lives inside of me and I would always hold this woman on a pedestal to keep the designer, the fashionista in me always inspired.....

CHAPTER 9

How to start your own label?

It was one of my dreams to craft my own fashion label. I started with a small store in the streets of Delhi's bazaars and it took me many years to reach where I am today. Even though the journey was not easy, there's no piece of it that I regret or wish it to be different. Because life is meant to teach you, it is meant to test you, pressurize you into giving up. But if there is one thing that you have made as your ultimate goal, the trials and tribulations of life only make the direction clearer, they never break the spine of a brave soldier. My struggles made my direction and my conviction crystal clear. I wanted to reach here, all my fights were to be where I am, the dream was to start the **Bhavana Singh** Label.

In today's time and age, we need immediate results. The next generations have forgotten the story of the rabbit and the turquoise, as most of the kids these days want to steadily jump steps in their journeys. Do you remember the quotations from Bhagavad Gita, "Karma karo par phal ki chinta mat karo". This saying defines what journey to building your own label is about.

Every iconic brand has an origin story. A clothing line that may dominate today's department stores may have started as a small business running out of an aspiring fashion designer's living room. While launching your own clothing line is challenging, thanks to ecommerce and online marketing, it just might be possible to turn a brand that began in a small online store into a clothing brand that's loved nationwide.

The great brands of the clothing industry were not built in a day. A lot of trial-and-error was involved, these brands almost certainly followed a business plan and continued to scale at a sustainable pace. There are going to be a lot of ups and downs, peaks and valleys but as I said before, always figure out the 'why' in your journey. This is the most important part. Once you are absolutely clear of why you want to do something, the 'how' and the 'what' resolves on its own. Starting a new company from scratch is never easy, but it's certainly possible. Remember that all of today's iconic brands started somewhere. It was the belief, the determination of the founders that brought their journeys to success.

Whatever I have learnt in my journey of crafting my own label, I have tried to summarize it in these ten starter points. And I hope they can help you to carve a path for yourself too.

1. **Identify a need in the market :** Remember that successful businesses often solve problems or fulfill needs for their customers. The same is true for a fashion label as well. By identifying a genuine need in the market, you can develop a product or service that has a higher likelihood of gaining traction and meeting the demands of your target audience. Conduct thorough market research to understand the current trends, consumer preferences, and gaps in the market.

- This is one of the reasons why I always say that don't rush establishing your label. It took me 17 long years to start my own Label. I know this is contradictory to what you commonly hear everywhere. But you can either trust someone who has spent years in this industry or just the fad of entrepreneurship.

- Crafting your own label is not just about clothes, it's about realizing your ideas into real life craft. Your clothes will only stand out if they are original art works and you need inspiration for that. Art is not a work of haste. Art has never been the work of haste. It requires years to come true, years to become worthy of showcasing. And as I said my art form tested my patience, tested my determination and my passion for years. Being an artist is not easy and this is why you should take time to build your basics. Take time to build your inspirations, to deeply understand the nature of your work and keep working towards excellence. Once you feel that you have gained enough experience in your field, it is then that you should think about going in the direction of a label.

- You identify a need when you know the plot. The more I worked with my clients, the more I understood what things they need the most, what is it that a layman struggles the most about when it comes to fashion. You need to understand the consumer and the art first. It's like the seeds of a plant are sown way before the tree bears fruit. Similarly a label cannot bear fruit until you plant the seed of observation. Observe your surroundings. Observe the clients, people, the markets you are working in. Align what you can offer and what the world needs and then lay the basis of something concrete.

2. **Develop a business plan :** No business can survive without a business plan. And this is where creative people mostly get stuck. You need to balance your creativity with the business aspect as well. Ultimately your label will survive because of its profitability which will come with a good business plan. This will guide your entire journey as a fashion designer and clothing manufacturer. Your business plan depends on the vision and the goals you have for your label. Do I want to be a brand name? Do I want to create a private label brand for a company? Do I want to create a premium brand that's sold in a boutique or Identify your goal and keep it foremost in your mind as you build your brand.

- Developing a business plan for your fashion label is a critical undertaking that requires a thoughtful and comprehensive approach. In the executive summary, succinctly articulate the core concept, mission, and unique selling proposition (USP) of your fashion label, outlining both short-term and long-term objectives. Provide a brief history and legal structure in the business description, and if applicable, specify the location of your business. Conduct a thorough market analysis to define your target audience, understand industry trends, and analyze competitors. Detail the structure of your team, emphasizing key roles and skills in the organization and management section. Outline your product or service line, delving into the design philosophy and unique features of your offerings.

- Moving to the marketing and sales strategy, clearly define your brand positioning and elaborate on your marketing plan, encompassing online presence, social media strategies, and potential collaborations. Articulate your sales strategy, be it through your own website, retail partnerships, or other channels. In the funding request section, present comprehensive financial projections, startup costs, and revenue forecasts, along with specifying the amount of funding sought and its intended use. Conduct a SWOT analysis to identify internal strengths and weaknesses, as well as external opportunities and threats. Additionally, recognize potential risks and outline strategies to mitigate them in the risk analysis section. Develop an implementation timeline that outlines key milestones and deadlines. In the appendices, include supporting documents such as market research data, resumes of key team members, or samples of your designs. Regularly update and seek feedback to ensure the ongoing relevance and effectiveness of your business plan.

3. **Identify your target audience :** This step is almost concurrent with number one. Your objective is not simply to identify a clothing item that should exist, but also the target market of consumers for that product. After all, brilliant design is of little use if it lacks potential customers. Consider the pros and cons of targeting certain demographics. For instance, young people tend to be style-conscious and may be more receptive to online marketing and word of mouth, but they also may have limited funds. Middle-aged customers may be able to afford a higher

price point, but they may be less concerned with style and already loyal to an existing brand identity. Identifying the target audience for our fashion label is a multifaceted process that involves a thorough understanding of demographics, psychographics, and behavioral characteristics. We aim to define our ideal customers in terms of age, gender, income, and geographic location, while also delving into their lifestyles, values, and interests. By exploring the activities and cultural influences that shape their choices, we can tailor our products and messaging to align with their preferences and aspirations. Understanding their shopping behaviors, brand loyalty, and engagement with fashion trends is crucial in crafting a strategy that resonates with them. Market research, including competitor analysis, provides insights into gaps and unique opportunities within the fashion landscape. Leveraging social media and online platforms, we assess the demographics of our followers and analyze how they interact with fashion-related content. Continuous engagement, feedback collection, and adaptability to evolving trends will refine our understanding of our audience, allowing our fashion label to create meaningful connections and deliver products that align seamlessly with their needs and desires.

4. **Start designing :** Embarking on the design process for your inaugural fashion collection is an opportunity to creatively showcase your unique vision while maintaining a practical approach to production. This transformative journey begins by defining a clear design philosophy that encapsulates your personal style and artistic identity. Extensive research and inspiration from various sources such as art, culture, and personal experiences will guide the creation of mood boards and sketches, forming the foundation of your collection. Identifying a central theme or concept unifies your designs, providing a cohesive narrative that resonates with your audience. Balancing creativity with practicality, carefully select materials and consider cost-effective manufacturing methods. Prototyping and sampling allow for refinement and adjustment, ensuring your designs are not only visually captivating

but also feasible in production. Integrating sustainable practices and seeking feedback from industry professionals contribute to the holistic development of your collection. Crafting a signature piece and presenting your designs through a captivating lookbook or presentation further enhances their impact. As you plan the launch and marketing strategy, remember that your first collection is a profound statement about your identity as a designer, and the delicate blend between the ideal and the attainable will pave the way for a successful and resonant debut in the fashion industry.

5. **Find a clothing manufacturer :** Finding a clothing manufacturer is a pivotal step for fashion entrepreneurs, unless they intend to personally handle the entire production process. The search for a manufacturing partner can take various forms, depending on the scale and nature of the fashion label. It could involve collaborating with colleagues in a home studio, sourcing fabric suppliers, or partnering with fully equipped factories capable of handling both limited boutique production and large-scale manufacturing

for established brands. Historically, clothing manufacturing has been predominantly situated outside the United States, leading many designers to explore partnerships in countries like China, Vietnam, Sri Lanka, or Bangladesh. While visiting the factory in person is ideal, budget constraints often compel new designers to conduct the entire vetting process through phone and email communications. For those with more modest fashion goals, such as adding a logo to existing streetwear, local options like print-on-demand screen printing facilities may offer a viable and cost-effective solution.

6. **Choose a brand name, logo, and market profile :** Once it's evident that your clothing items can be manufactured with reasonable production costs, the next crucial step is crafting your brand's public profile. This involves selecting a business name that resonates with your identity, designing a distinctive logo, and, if applicable, creating a memorable slogan. Building a cohesive and visually appealing website using e-commerce platforms like Shopify or Etsy is imperative for reaching your audience. Consider

incorporating a compelling narrative into your brand elements, be it in the brand name, logo, or website, as customers are often drawn to brands with authentic and engaging stories. It's essential to complete this branding work concurrently with the manufacturing process, ensuring that your public presence is ready by the time your clothing items are produced. This strategic alignment allows for a seamless transition to selling your goods as soon as they are made, maximizing the impact of your brand in the market.

7. **Choose a price point for your items :** Selecting the right price point for your clothing items is a crucial step in the establishment of your fashion business and should align closely with your understanding of the target audience. Consider setting a price that not only covers production costs but also resonates with the financial capacity and preferences of your potential customers. It's essential to strike a balance between maintaining profitability and ensuring accessibility to the market. Understanding the economic demographics, purchasing behavior, and lifestyle of your target audience

will guide you in determining a price point that neither compromises the perceived value of your products nor alienates the customers necessary for the successful launch of your fashion venture. This strategic approach fosters a pricing strategy that not only sustains your business but also establishes a positive relationship with your audience, laying the foundation for long-term success.

8. **Begin the marketing process:** Commencing the marketing process for your budding fashion label is a pivotal step to establish brand awareness and capture the attention of potential customers. Utilizing platforms like Instagram has become a popular and effective strategy in the modern landscape. Leverage the visual appeal of your fashion creations by showcasing them on Instagram, a platform widely embraced for its visual-centric nature. I too am active on my social profiles and I have found it to be a great way to connect with your potential customers. In fact, my first client ever had also reached out to me on my instagram profile. Collaborate with Instagram influencers who align with your brand aesthetics and target audience.

Many influencers are open to promoting new fashion brands in exchange for your products, providing a cost-effective means to amplify your brand's reach. Crafting engaging and shareable content, such as behind-the-scenes glimpses, styling tips, or exclusive previews, enhances your brand's visibility. Additionally, consider investing in other digital marketing channels, such as Facebook, Pinterest, and Google Ads, to diversify your online presence and attract a broader audience. This multifaceted approach will contribute to building a robust brand presence and fostering initial interest as your fashion label takes its first steps into the competitive market.

9. **Set realistic sales and distribution goals:** Setting realistic sales and distribution goals for your fashion label is a critical aspect of ensuring sustainable growth, and seeking the assistance of a business professional can be instrumental in navigating this complex terrain. While your fashion vision is the heart of your brand, understanding the intricacies of clothing distribution requires expertise that extends beyond design. Collaborating

with a business professional or consultant with experience in fashion retail can provide invaluable insights into market trends, consumer behavior, and effective distribution strategies. Establishing achievable sales goals is essential for gauging your label's performance against your business plan and ensuring steady progress. A professional's guidance can help you align your sales and distribution objectives with industry benchmarks and realistic growth trajectories. Overcoming the fear of seeking assistance in this realm can ultimately contribute to the success of your fashion label, allowing you to navigate the intricacies of sales and distribution with a strategic and informed approach.

10. **Start a soft launch, and then look for more Investment and partnerships:** Once you've successfully established a proof of concept with clothing ready for limited sales, the next strategic step is about involving potential business partners and co-investors. While the idea of sole ownership and full control over future profits may be appealing, the reality of scaling a business often necessitates access

to additional capital. Opting for a business partner who can inject capital into the venture in exchange for a share of future proceeds is a conventional and effective approach. This collaborative model allows for the infusion of resources needed for growth, whether it be expanding production capabilities, reaching new markets, or investing in marketing initiatives. It's a pragmatic way to secure the financial support required for scaling up, acknowledging that partnerships and co-investors play a pivotal role in the journey from a proof of concept to a thriving and sustainable fashion label.

Building a label is not for everyone. It is a work of patience and requires a person's original ideas. The more time you take to reach the top the better you become at holding that top position. When you know your work and the market inside out there is very little that can stop you from making full use of the opportunities that will arise on the journey. Live your life in a way that whatever you do, you look at, you listen to, inspire your work too. And before starting the business, learn the skills that are required to run the business. Learning will never let you down. It's one thing that no one can take away from you and it is yours for the rest of your life. Don't be afraid of failures but always try to make unique mistakes,and learn from the ones others have already committed. Your unique journey should become a part of what you are building and it should speak of you without you even uttering a word in its explanation.

CHAPTER 10

Is talent enough to survive the fashion industry?

Talent is the first marker that decides if you are suitable to work in a creative industry like fashion or not. It is crucial in the fashion world because it's the creative engine that drives new ideas and makes the industry stand out. Creative people with talent bring fresh and unique perspectives, keeping the industry always changing and exciting. If you don't have talent, there is nothing to start with. Talent is like a foundation upon which you can begin to build the structure of your career. But is talent enough to reach the heights of success in this industry? You'll find out in this chapter.

These are the names that are known to almost everyone. These people made it big in their fields because they did a combination of so many things. For sure they had talent but they also added some extra factors that took them where they are today.

- Ritesh Agarwal, CEO of OYO Rooms
- Gautam Adani, Chairman of Adani Group
- Bill Gates, Co-founder of Microsoft
- Michael Dell, CEO of Dell Technologies

- Mark Zuckerberg, CEO of Facebook
- Steve Jobs, Founder of Apple

Even though these founders belong to a mix of fields, there were certain common traits that can be traced back to each one of them. Firstly, these leaders all possessed a clear vision and were innovative in their approaches. Whether creating new markets or revolutionizing existing ones, they demonstrated a forward-thinking mindset that set them apart. Their ability to envision and work towards long-term goals played a pivotal role in their success.

Secondly, persistence and resilience were inherent traits in these leaders. They faced setbacks and challenges along their entrepreneurial journeys but displayed unwavering determination to overcome obstacles. Learning from failures and using them as stepping stones to success was a shared characteristic.

Adaptability stands out as another key factor. The business landscape is dynamic, and successful leaders adapt to changing circumstances. Technological advancements, shifts in consumer behavior, or evolving market trends were met with a readiness to adapt and evolve.

Whether it was providing affordable accommodation (OYO), developing user-friendly software (Microsoft), or creating innovative tech products (Apple, Dell, Facebook), customer satisfaction was a priority.

Risk-taking, a hallmark of entrepreneurial success, was embraced by these leaders. They took calculated risks, made strategic decisions, and were unafraid of venturing into uncharted territories that led to significant advancements in their respective industries.

Their innovative mindsets that were solution oriented also played a crucial role in their success. They introduced or embraced disruptive business models that challenged traditional industry norms. A long-term vision was evident in all of their journeys. Beyond short-term gains, these leaders considered the sustainability and growth of their ventures over time, emphasizing the importance of thinking beyond immediate successes.

Most importantly, recognizing the importance of giving back to society, they leveraged their success to make a positive impact beyond their business endeavors.

In essence, the success of Ritesh Agarwal, Gautam Adani, Bill Gates, Michael Dell, Mark Zuckerberg, and Steve Jobs was not just about talent, it involves so much more.

So let's first address the question, which is more important degree or skill?

Coco Chanel, the founder of one of the biggest brands of our times going by the same name, did not have a formal degree in fashion or a related field. Unlike many contemporary designers, she did not receive formal academic training in design or fashion. Chanel was born in 1883 in Saumur, France, and she grew up in an orphanage after the death of her mother. Her early life involved various jobs, including working as a seamstress and a singer.

Coco Chanel's entry into the fashion world was through her work as a milliner (hat maker) in the early 20th century. She gained attention for her elegant and innovative hat designs, which eventually led to the opening of her own boutique in Paris.

Chanel's impact on the fashion industry was significant despite her lack of formal education in the field. Her designs were revolutionary, and she played a crucial role in changing women's fashion by introducing more comfortable, practical, and modern clothing. The Chanel brand became synonymous with timeless elegance and sophistication. Coco Chanel is credited with popularizing the "little black dress," introducing casual chic through her use of jersey fabric, and creating the timeless Chanel suit. Her designs were characterized by simplicity, elegance, and a focus on functionality. Chanel's influence extended beyond clothing, as she also introduced the now-iconic Chanel No. 5 perfume.

Apart from her innovative designs, Coco Chanel's success can be attributed to her entrepreneurial spirit, resilience, talent and determination. She transformed her small hat shop into a global fashion empire. Chanel's legacy continues to shape the fashion industry, and her impact is still evident in the enduring popularity of the Chanel brand and the timeless aesthetic she brought to women's fashion.

On the other hand, one example of an individual who has made a significant impact in the Indian fashion industry with a formal degree is **Manish Malhotra**. Manish Malhotra is a renowned Indian fashion designer and costume stylist who has played a pivotal role in shaping the country's fashion landscape.

Manish Malhotra studied at Elphinstone College in Mumbai, where he pursued a degree in Arts. While his initial academic background was not specifically in fashion design, he had a keen interest in the field. After completing his education, he started his career as a model and ventured into the fashion industry.

However, Manish Malhotra's breakthrough came when he transitioned to costume designing for Bollywood films. His talent for creating stunning and innovative costumes caught the attention of the film industry, and he soon became one of the most sought-after costume designers in Bollywood. Over time, he expanded his repertoire to include designing for celebrities, high-profile events, and his own fashion label.

Manish Malhotra's success illustrates how a combination of talent, formal education, and industry experience can lead to significant achievements in the fashion world. His journey from studying arts to becoming a celebrated fashion designer and stylist showcases the impact of skills honed through experience and a foundation in the arts on a successful career in the Indian fashion industry.

Therefore to Answer

Is Talent Enough for Success in Fashion?

I am a prime example that represents the side, "talent is more important than a degree". I didn't have any formal education in the field, or in any other field for that sake. I have been more of an intuitive stylist, I trust my guts to tell me what fits well in fashion and what doesn't. It's a sense I was born with and then I worked hard to inculcate and develop it even further. So, if you look at my life's example, you can very well advocate for the dictum that talent is more important than a degree.

But is it always true? There are so many other examples as one accounted for above, that will show you the leverage that a degree from a good institute brings to you. Students from some of the leading fashion institutes of India are indeed leading the world.

This is why I want to say that there is no single path to be followed in life, it is a ferry on merry-go-arounds that can take us from anywhere to anywhere. Life is an open adventure for everyone to experience. For some people fail even if they come from the highest qualification background and for some people succeed even if they come from nothing. What defines your success is nothing external, it is the clarity of thought, direction and effort that takes you somewhere.When you know what you want the forces of the universe conspire to bring it to you. As said, "figure out the why and the what and the universe will figure out the how." See, degrees cannot provide the answer to what you want and why you want it, it is one of the paths that you can take to pursue the ambition that you run towards. There are many ways to pursue your goals and I think a degree from the top institute makes it fairly easy for you to reach where you wanna go. It brings the resources, networks, opportunities to you.

But there is a trend in our country that teaches us to run after degrees. It teaches us that degrees are the only way through which we can enter the professional world and be successful. This is where it gets a little out of the line.

Dreams see no class, no boundaries, no background. And all walks of people have the right to pursue what they want. But for a person who doesn't come from a strong financial background, higher education of course becomes challenging. I would say that because of the democratization of careers and industries, things have changed even in the fashion industry as well. Before this, fashion was considered as an unwelcoming place that needed fortunes or connections to even begin with.

For me personally, the longing to learn more about fashion and styling was the reason that I stand here without quitting on my passion. My curiosity knew no bounds, I didn't care if I was learning from a formal or an informal source, education is education, no matter the source that it comes from.

I think the scope of this topic goes far beyond degree and skills, because to survive and succeed in the real world, you need more than just a degree or a skill. Fashion is a highly competitive industry. Getting your foot to the threshold of the fashion world is challenging. It's an extremely desirable industry to work in, which means it's equally as competitive.

Often seen as a glamorous industry to work in, the reality is that it takes a lot of hard work, dedication, creativity and innovative thinking.

CHAPTER 11

Ten lessons from my life

1. **Make your business your lifestyle:** Business is all about passion. Passion drives you to forget about everything else and just focus on the mission of your life. If your passion doesn't let you sleep, doesn't let you fall off easily, you are in the right direction. But the most important thing to consider here is that all the hard work in this direction is inspired work, you feel good about the work that you do. Whereas if you just do something for money or for the sake of doing it, you are not building a business, you are building a cage for yourself. When you dedicate your time, your effort to something, your energy levels replenish from the joy you feel by imbibing the hard work into your life. You can do so much more because what you are doing at the time, it makes you happy, it gives you energy to do way beyond the ordinary. However, when you work out of compulsion or half heartedness, your energy reciprocates by resisting the work. This is why I say if you want to build a business, build it around the work that you can incorporate into your everyday life. For me, my work is my happiness and this is why I can dedicate more

and more part of my life to it and this time commitment helps me grow my business even further. If your work doesn't make you happy, you will find excuses to reduce the amount of time you have to spend doing it, and your business will obviously suffer from your absence. A lot of entrepreneurs think that will set the business and leave it to their employees to run, but that is never the case, you have to be the first person who cares about the business the most, it's your brainchild not someone else's.

2. **Client comes first:** The person who pays for the services that your company provides, is the client and client should always be kept first. There needs to be made an effort to make the client comfortable, heard, and provide them a safe space to open to. If a client comes to you with a certain problem and you don't bring them with a solution that suits their needs, you are of no use to them. Imagine that you go to a store and it has been your favorite one since your childhood. All your favorite toys came from this store. And now you too are with a child and you wanna relive those memories by visiting the place.

But the sales staff in that store sees you as a mere customer and even after describing the context of your visit, no one pays attention to the story, rather they push you to buy stuff from the store. How will this make you feel? You will feel that your value is only the money that you have in your pocket, and you are nothing more to them than a sales target. This example is what is to be kept in mind while dealing with clients. They are not just money tags, they are real people with real issues that you are proposing to solve. Treat them as family, value their feedback and listen to what they have to say.

Don't make them feel that their stories are not important, each detail of their life that they rightly share is important for your work, especially in an industry like fashion where stories and personalities are what inspire the work of an artist. Other than this, satisfied customers are more likely to become repeat customers and champions for your business. Meeting their needs and expectations can help you get more business by positive reviews and word-of-mouth referrals. By providing excellent service and prioritizing client needs, you encourage repeat business. When clients feel valued and prioritized, they are more likely to develop loyalty to your brand and loyalty often leads to long-term relationships, reducing the need for constant marketing efforts to attract new clients.

3. **Work smart :** Working smart is like finding the best and easiest way to get things done. It's not just about working hard, but about using your brain to make tasks easier and quicker. When you work smart, you focus on the most important things first and use your time wisely. This helps you achieve your goals faster without feeling too tired or stressed. It's like figuring out the shortcuts that make your work more efficient. By working smart, you not only save time but also make sure you do a great job. It's a smart way to balance your work and personal life, keeping you happy and successful in the long run. So, instead of just putting in a lot of effort, try to work smart to make things easier and more enjoyable!

Just the hardwork will not take you anywhere, today you require to be street smart. You are required to know how to scale, how to deal with things happening both inside and outside your work and these things will only come when you are open to learn with an open mind. Most people think that they know it all, that they are the best at what they do. But being smart is about recognizing that you can learn from anyone, you can learn from any situation and turn failures into successes. Being smart is about not letting anyone make use of the hard work that you do. It's like a protective shield that will guard you against the manipulations and the pitfalls that come in the life of a businesswoman.

4. **Making Profit is important:** A lot of people will tell you that passion is about following your dreams and money is secondary, and all that. But I am telling you if your passion is making you money, only then you are moving in the right direction. Otherwise someone else is using your talent, your skills and making money off of it. So, it's one thing to be philanthropic but no philanthropy should come out of you getting exploited for someone else's benefit. Therefore, pay a lot of attention to your finances. Keep a track on where the money is coming from, where is it going to, how much are you

allotting to expenses, how much are you saving and how much are you reinvesting in the business. Learn what ratios will best suit your business and then take actions to correct and streamline, if there is something that is going wrong. Moreover, being financially aware allows you to strike a balance between pursuing your passion and ensuring a sustainable livelihood. It's not just about making money; it's about making informed decisions to safeguard your creative and professional pursuits. By actively tracking your income sources and understanding your expenditures, you empower yourself to make strategic choices. Being good with money also helps when talking to investors or making deals. It's like having a superpower that makes your business strong and able to handle challenges.

4. **Be very clear about what you offer to people:** A value proposition, your offer, is like the special thing that makes customers want to choose your business. Imagine you're in a candy store, and there are many candies to choose from. Your value proposition is like saying, "Our candy is sugar free and made

from natural ingredients!" It helps customers looking for sugar-free natural candies, understand why your business is right for them. It's not just about selling a product or service.

For me I don't like to call myself a stylist because I feel this label kind of limits the scope of the work that I do for my clients. And it doesn't justify the work that I do. I mind perceiving more about the role through a tag than they do with describing the role. It's concise information that is very easy to digest for us. Plus the labels of professions that we use have met with equally long lasting descriptions of their corresponding job roles. And it becomes difficult to challenge these notions. This is why I refrain from calling myself a stylist. Styling is a part of my job, it is not entirely what I do. I help people transform and yes fashion is a big part of it. It does two things with this, one I widen the scope of my relationship with the client and two I make my value proposition very clear by defining what I do in a line.

If you are confused about what you do, your clients are going to be equally or even more confused. Business works on clarity of value propositions. Know what you are offering and make it crystal clear. A person should know who you are, what you do and what value you will offer to them. If you don't like the label, the one liners that exist regarding what you do, change them and use them to suit your needs, use them to suit your voice and your work.

6. **Resilience is the key to success:** Resilience is like having a superpower that helps you bounce back and stay strong when faced with challenges or tough times. It's the ability to adapt and keep going, even when things get difficult. In real life, it's about not giving up when you face problems or setbacks. We are taught that failures are bad, that failures shall be avoided at all costs. But failures actually test how important your set goal is for you. How important is this thing that you have been running after. It gives you multiple chances to quit and if you don't like anything, it shows you the possibility that you can look for something else. But if what you are after

is important to you, it's a matter of life or death for you, no matter how many failures come your way, you will not have it in you to leave and quit. Failure opens two gates, CONTINUE OR QUIT. If it's important you continue and if not you quit. And to continue you need resilience. It helps you learn from tough situations, grow stronger, and keep moving forward. Resilience is what helps you pick up the blocks and try again, learning from each attempt. In the journey toward success, there are often challenges, failures, or unexpected twists. Resilience is the key because it allows you to bounce back from setbacks, stay determined, and keep moving forward.

Life will keep putting you through a rollercoaster with twists and turns. When you're resilient, you can handle the twists better. It doesn't mean you won't feel sad or disappointed, but resilience helps you cope and find solutions. It's like having an inner strength that keeps you going, no matter what challenges come your way. So, in the big adventure of life, resilience is your trusty sidekick, helping you navigate and survive the journey.

7. **Know your audience:** One thing that I ask my clients before giving them a style makeover or before designing clothes is to know the the places they frequent, their average everyday, the kind of company they keep, the kind of events they attend and the venues they visit. This information helps me to learn about their audience. See, fashion is a statement. It says a lot about you, without you uttering a word. So, you should always know your audience. You can't make a bold statement where it would make you stand out but in a poor taste. For someone in fashion, knowing your audience is like having a fashion compass that guides your style choices. Imagine you're designing clothes or showcasing a new collection – understanding your audience helps you create something they'll love and relate to. Fashion is all about expressing a message through clothing, and knowing your audience ensures that your message resonates with them.Different people have different tastes, preferences, and styles. Knowing your audience means understanding what colors, designs, or trends they prefer. It's like tailoring your creations

to fit their unique fashion sensibilities. This knowledge is essential for fashion designers, retailers, or influencers because it helps them connect with their audience on a deeper level. Whether you're selling clothes, creating a fashion brand, or influencing style trends, knowing your audience allows you to speak their fashion language. It's about creating a connection and making your fashion choices relatable and appealing to the people you want to reach. So, in the world of fashion, knowing your audience is like having the perfect accessory – it completes your look and makes your style truly stand out.

8. **Personal style has a say:** Personal style refers to the different ways in which individuals express themselves especially through clothing, accessories, grooming, and overall appearance. It reflects a person's unique preferences, taste, and identity. Personal style is not just about following fashion trends but involves a deeper understanding of one's personality, lifestyle, and individual preferences. It plays a significant role in the fashion industry, not only for fashion designers but also for anyone involved in the

field. Developing a unique and recognizable personal style helps individuals stand out in a crowded industry. Whether it's a preference for bold colors, avant-garde designs, or a specific silhouette, having a distinct identity can make a lasting impression. For fashion designers who wear their own designs, their personal style becomes a visual representation of their brand. It serves as a walking advertisement and can attract attention from potential clients, collaborators, or investors. Fashion is a form of art, and personal style allows individuals to express their creativity. It's a way to communicate ideas, emotions, and concepts without saying a word. Originality is always the trendsetter and when aesthetics resonate with a broader audience, it brings revolutions.

8. **Don't forget the why:** In the hustle of day-to-day operations, it's easy to get caught up in the 'what' and 'how' of our business. But, let's not forget the heartbeat, the essence, the 'why' that kick started this incredible journey. Our 'why' is more than a mission statement; it's the driving force that breathes life into every decision, every innovation,

and every interaction. It's the passion that fuels our commitment to excellence. When the challenges seem insurmountable, and the goals appear distant, it's the 'why' that steadies our course. It's the reason we started this journey, the purpose that transcends profit margins and market share. Customers don't just buy what we do; they buy why we do it. So, it's important to weave our 'why' into the fabric of everything we create - from products to customer experiences. It's the authenticity in our 'why' that resonates with our audience and turns them into our rightful advocates.

10. **Keep it real:** This is for everyone, whether you are a stylist reading this, a student, a designer, a woman looking for change in her life, this is for each one of you. Remember that in this ever-evolving world of fashion - staying true to yourself is the most important thing. Your personal style is your signature, and it speaks louder than you might think. Don't get lost in the trends or conform to the industry's expectations if it doesn't align with who you are. Your authenticity is your superpower. It's what catches the eye, sparks

conversations, and opens doors you never thought possible. Whether you're rocking your own designs or curating a wardrobe that screams "you" - keep it real. Embrace the quirks, celebrate the uniqueness, and let your style tell a story. In a world that can sometimes feel like a runway, remember, the most compelling fashion statement is the one that feels genuine.

Here's to staying true, standing out, and making waves with an authentic flair.

Regards

Bhavana Singh.